CH

D0624886

THE **HUMAN** MICROBIOME:
THE GERMS THAT KEEP YOU HEALTHY

REBECCA E. HIRSCH

THE
HUMAN
MICRO

BIOME

THE GERMS THAT
KEEP YOU HEALTHY

REBECCA E. HIRSCH

TWENTY FIRST CENTURY BOOKS / MINNEAPOLIS

To my mother, Donna Jean Stange, a dedicated nurse who taught me that a little dirt is good for the immune system

Twenty-First Century Books
A division of Lerner Publishing Group, Inc.
241 First Avenue North
Minneapolis, MN 55401 USA

For reading levels and more information, look up this title at www.lernerbooks.com.

Main body text set in Adrianna Regular 11/15
Typeface provided by Chank.

Library of Congress Cataloging-in-Publication Data

Hirsch, Rebecca E., author.
    The Human Microbiome: The Germs That Keep You Healthy/ Rebecca E. Hirsch.
        pages cm
    Includes bibliographical references and index.
    ISBN 978-1-4677-8568-6 (lb : alk. paper) — ISBN 978-1-5124-1140-9 (eb pdf)
    1. Human body—Microbiology—Juvenile literature. 2. Medical microbiology—Juvenile literature. 3. Drug resistance in microorganisms—Juvenile literature.
    I. Title.
    QR171.A1H57 2017
    612—dc23   2015014264

Manufactured in the United States of America
1 – DP – 7/15/16

CONTENTS

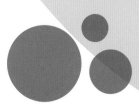

THE HUMAN ECOSYSTEM

Look in the mirror and what do you see? Do you notice the color of your eyes, the shape of your nose, or the pimple that erupted only yesterday on your chin? Look again, and this time, try to imagine the parts of yourself that you can't see.

On your face right now are millions of creatures invisible to the naked eye. These tiny living things, called microbes, call *you* home. They squirm across your cheeks, flourish on your forehead, and nestle inside your nostrils. You'll also find them in the moist pockets of your armpits, the dry crooks of your elbows, and your lint-speckled navel. Vast cities of them thrive in the dark, damp environment of your large intestine.

That person you see in the mirror? Your body is made of more than just human cells. Trillions and trillions of cells on and inside your body are microbes. Microbial cells are tiny compared to human cells, so your microbiome—the collection of microbes on and in you—weighs only between 2 and 5 pounds (0.9–2.3 kilograms), a fraction of your body weight. If the thought of 2 to 5 pounds of microbes has you longing for a hot shower, you are doing what people have done for a long time: thinking of microbes as unhealthy germs and trying to scrub them away. But you couldn't rid your body of these bugs, even if you tried. And that's a good thing. Most of our tiny tenants don't make us sick. They belong on our bodies. They moved in the moment we were born and have been living there, performing essential jobs for us, ever since.

Microbes live in your nose and lungs, on your skin, in your mouth and gut (the stomach and the intestines), and in your urogenital (excretion and reproduction) tract. Some parts of you have few microbes. Other parts are thickly coated. The microbes in some body parts are very diverse, with hundreds of different species living side by side. Other areas have less diversity, with just a few different kinds of microbes.

In total, the human body holds thousands of different kinds of microbes. You have many in common with the person sitting next to you in math class—and even more in common with the people

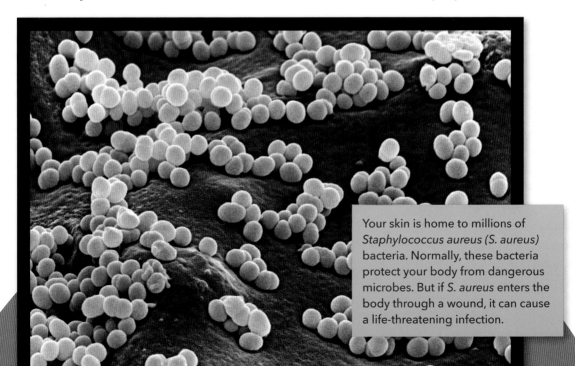

Your skin is home to millions of *Staphylococcus aureus (S. aureus)* bacteria. Normally, these bacteria protect your body from dangerous microbes. But if *S. aureus* enters the body through a wound, it can cause a life-threatening infection.

in your family. But your overall mix is unique, like a fingerprint. Your personal set of microbes has been influenced by many aspects of your life, including the traits you inherited from your parents, what foods you eat, what medicines you take, and where you live. Altogether, these microbes shape human health in ways scientists are just beginning to understand.

You can think of the microbiome collectively as a hidden organ, one that scientists didn't discover until the late twentieth century. This organ helps digest your food and provides essential nutrients, such as vitamin K, which plays a role in blood clotting but is not made by your own cells. The microbiome trains the immune system—the cells and tissues in your body that fight off disease—helping that system develop and work properly. The microbiome crowds out harmful microbes that could make you sick. It even shapes your behavior. Changes in this organ have been linked to a wide range of diseases—from asthma and allergies to obesity,

THE LOWDOWN ON MICROBES

- Microbes are in the air you breathe, the ground you walk on, the food you eat, and your body.
- Roughly one hundred billion microbes live on your skin. There are more microbes on your hand than there are people on the entire planet (7.4 billion).
- Your intestines house more bacteria than anywhere else in your body, up to five hundred billion microbes per teaspoon (5 milliliters) of fluid.
- By one recent estimate, your body is home to thirty-seven trillion human cells and about the same number of microbes, although the exact ratio probably varies from person to person.

autism, and autoimmune disorders (diseases in which the immune system attacks healthy cells).

The quest to understand this organ is changing how doctors, scientists, and researchers think about health and the human body. Scientists are discovering the great extent to which microbes influence our health and well-being. They are learning that each of us is a superorganism: a complex, dynamic blend of microbial cells and human cells, all working together as a single living thing.

A LIVING NETWORK

To understand the complex relationships between your microbes and the rest of your body, it helps to think like an ecologist. Ecology is the branch of science that deals with the relationship between organisms and their environment. Just as a tropical forest includes trees, flowers, vines, mammals, birds, amphibians, reptiles, and insects living and working together, our bodies include tiny creatures that live and work alongside our human cells.

The body is an ecosystem, a complex blend of different kinds of organisms living together. In the human ecosystem, microbes interact with their human hosts, with one another, and with the environment inside the body. To be even more accurate, the body is not just one ecosystem. It is a series of ecosystems. We can compare it to a jungle, in which different animals occupy different places and play different roles in the living environment. Certain insects, birds, and mammals live high in the sunlit treetops. Drop to the forest floor and turn over a log. You'll find completely different species living there: millipedes, centipedes, insects, and slugs. So it is with microbes on your body. One bunch lives in your warm, moist nostril. A different crew occupies your dry, smooth forearm. Many more live in other parts of your body.

The human microbiome is diverse. Diversity refers to the number of different species in an environment. The Amazon rain forest in South America has high diversity, with roughly sixteen thousand different species of trees. But travel to the Sonoran Desert in the US Southwest and northwestern Mexico, and you'll find fewer types of trees, or lower diversity. The microbiome is similar. Some parts of you are more diverse than others. Your forearm, for instance, hosts many more microbial species than the crease behind your ear.

Two more concepts from ecology apply to the microbiome: extinction and collapse. Just as certain species of plants or animals in a tropical forest can become extinct—or die out completely—so too can microbes in your body. In nature, loss of diversity or even the loss of one key species can lead to collapse, or permanent and lasting damage to an ecosystem. An example is the loss of wolves from Yellowstone National Park in Wyoming, Idaho, and Montana. Wolves disappeared from the park (and most of the western United States) in the 1930s, after years of being killed by hunters, ranchers, and farmers. Without the wolves that normally preyed on elks, the park's elk population grew. The elks fed on young willow, aspen, and cottonwood trees, which beavers use for food and to build dams to make ponds. With fewer trees, the park's beavers could not survive. Without beavers, beaver ponds disappeared, along with the plants and animals that lived in and around the ponds—and the repercussions continued along the food chain. In this way, with the loss of one species, the entire Yellowstone ecosystem became unbalanced. This can happen to the human microbiome as well. Lack of diversity of the body's microbes, or the loss of particular microbial species, has been associated with an increased risk of health problems, including obesity, infection, allergies, and immune malfunction.

RELATIONSHIPS IN THE MICROBE JUNGLE

The complex relationship between microbes and humans is the product of millions of years of evolution—the process by which living organisms change over time. The evolution of two or more closely associated species is called coevolution. In coevolution several species change together, each one shaping the other's evolution. As a result of a long period of coevolution between humans and microbes, we have come to depend on microbes for certain parts of our biology, including digestion of food and the development of our immune systems. In return, microbes have come to depend on humans for food and a protected place to live.

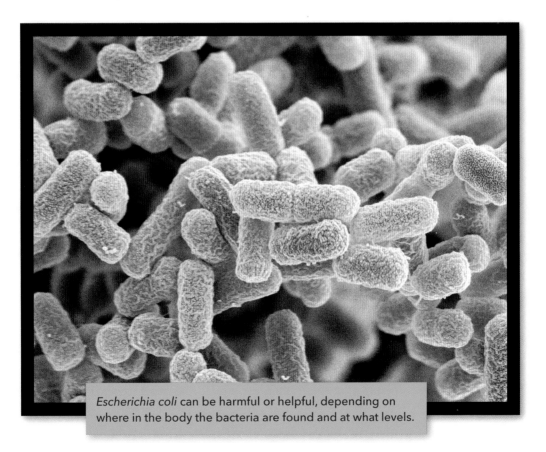

Escherichia coli can be harmful or helpful, depending on where in the body the bacteria are found and at what levels.

YOU NAME IT

Scientists label every recognized species on Earth with a two-part scientific name. This system for naming species, called binomial nomenclature, was invented by Swedish botanist Carolus Linnaeus in the eighteenth century.

The first part of a scientific name, which is capitalized, labels a category called a genus. All organisms within a genus are closely related. Lions and tigers both belong to the genus *Panthera*. The second part of the scientific name, in lowercase, identifies the particular species to which an organism belongs, separate from all other species. Lions are the species *Panthera leo*. Tigers are *Panthera tigris*. Both parts of the scientific name are italicized.

As with the names of plants and animals, microbial names follow the rules of binomial nomenclature. The bacterial species *Staphylococcus aureus* belongs to the genus *Staphylococcus*. The species is related to but distinct from the species *Staphylococcus epidermidis*. Sometimes species names are abbreviated, with the genus indicated by only a capital letter. In this system, *Staphylococcus aureus* becomes *S. aureus*.

Some microbes benefit their human hosts and receive some benefit in return. These microbes are known as mutualists. Many microbes found in the human gut are mutualists. We give them food and a place to live, and in return, they help digest our food and fight harmful bacteria in the gut. Some microbes benefit from living inside our bodies, but they do not help or harm us. These microbes are called commensals. Think of commensal microbes as harmless hitchhikers. Many microbes found in the nose and sinuses are commensals. A third group contains the microbes that get most of the attention: pathogens, the ones that cause disease. They grow and benefit at our expense. Compared to mutualists and commensals, pathogens are rare. They make up only a tiny fraction of the microbes in our bodies.

Keep in mind that microbes often don't fit neatly into just one category. Some microbes can help us in some circumstances and harm us in others. For example, *Staphylococcus aureus* normally lives on the skin, where it keeps invading pathogens away. It is normally a mutualist. But if it enters the body through a wound, it can become a pathogen, leading to severe illness and even death. At low levels, *Escherichia coli* in the gut keeps out harmful bacteria. But at high levels or found elsewhere inside the body, it can cause diarrhea or a deadly infection. Again and again, scientists see that a single microbe can be both a helper and a killer, beneficial in one situation but dangerous in another.

2

PLANET OF THE MICROBES

Microbes dominate life on Earth. Microbes may be small, but they are many. If you could gather together the billions and billions of microbes, they would outweigh all the visible life-forms on the planet—all the fish in the sea, the trees in the forest, and the humans, whales, elephants, mice, birds, and plants combined.

Microbes are invisible, but they are powerful and they make life on Earth possible. Outside the human body, microbes help digest dead plants and animals, breaking them down into soil, in which new plants will grow. In this way, microbes are vital to food webs everywhere. Microbes perform such essential services that all other creatures would die without them. "It's clear to me that if you wiped all multicellular life-forms off the face of the earth, microbial life might shift a tiny bit," said University of Illinois microbiologist Carl Woese. "[But] if microbial life were to disappear, that would be it—instant death for the planet."

Microbes are too small to see, but you can see their effects in the natural world. For instance, microbes are feeding on these rotting vegetables, breaking them down into nutrient-rich soil.

Invisible Life

What are microbes exactly? Scientists define a microbe as any organism too small to be seen with the naked eye. That's a very large group. It includes three dramatically different types of living things: bacteria, archaea, and eukaryotes. A fourth category, viruses, is also part of the human microbiome, although strictly speaking, viruses are not alive.

Bacteria

Bacteria are prokaryotes, single-celled organisms with no compartments inside their cells. They come in a few different shapes. Bacilli are rod-shaped. Cocci are shaped like balls. Spirochetes are curvy corkscrews.

Bacterial cells are surrounded by a cell membrane (also called a plasma membrane), which is in turn surrounded by a semirigid cell wall. Bacterial genes—units of heredity containing instructions on how bacteria will live and reproduce—are encoded on a single chromosome, a loop of deoxyribonucleic acid (DNA).

This loop floats freely in the cell. Some bacteria also contain small circles of DNA called plasmids.

Bacteria can be classified as gram-positive or gram-negative. Gram-positive bacteria turn purple in a Gram stain test, a test that scientists use to identify types of bacteria. Because of the structure of their cell walls, gram-positive bacteria take up the violet dye used in the test. Gram-negative bacteria have a different kind of cell wall and fail to take up the dye.

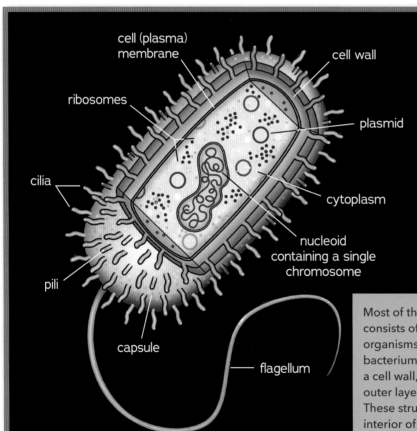

cell (plasma) membrane

cell wall

ribosomes

plasmid

cilia

cytoplasm

pili

nucleoid containing a single chromosome

capsule

flagellum

Most of the human microbiome consists of single-celled organisms called bacteria. Each bacterium has a cell membrane, a cell wall, and sometimes an outer layer called a capsule. These structures protect the interior of the cell. Inside, the cell contains ribosomes, plasmids, and a loop of chromosome inside a region called a nucleoid. These components allow the cell to reproduce and pass on traits to its offspring. Pili, cilia, and flagella help bacterial cells move.

DEEP TIME

Microbes have lived on Earth for roughly 3.7 billion years. Modern humans (*Homo sapiens*) have lived on Earth for only about 200,000 years. Scientists use the term *deep time* to describe vast stretches of time—going so far back that they are difficult for us to grasp. One way to wrap our minds around these long stretches of time is to compare them to a length of time we can easily understand, such as a single, twenty-four-hour day. If the history of life on Earth were condensed into one day, microbes would be present for all of it. Modern humans would appear at about two seconds before midnight.

Bacteria may be simple and single-celled, but they are savvy survivors. They evolve at breathtaking speed, adapting to new environments and giving rise to new species like branches sprouting on a tree. As a result, they are a highly diverse group. They are found in every habitat on Earth. They live high in the clouds and in the deep, dark ocean. They live on rocks and in soil and on the roots of some plants. They live on and inside animals, including you. Bacteria make up the bulk of your microbiome.

ARCHAEA

Archaea are microscopic, single-celled organisms that look a lot like bacteria. Like bacteria, they are prokaryotes. They have a cell membrane and a semirigid cell wall. They lack cell compartments, and their genetic material is a loop of DNA. Although archaea look similar to bacteria, appearances can be deceiving.

Archaea often behave differently than bacteria. Some archaea belch methane, the main component of natural gas. Some thrive in extreme environments—sweltering hot springs, super-salty lakes, or petroleum deposits deep underground—although archaea can inhabit non-extreme environments too. Archaea are present in your microbiome but in much smaller numbers than bacteria. Microbiologists identified archaea in the 1970s, and at first, scientists thought these bacteria look-alikes were just weird bacteria. But scientists have learned that archaea are a distinct kind of organism and are not closely related to bacteria. Although they appear similar, archaea and bacteria differ in important ways. For instance, archaea build their cell membranes and cell walls with different chemicals than bacteria do. Archaea may actually be more closely related to eukaryotes, the third group of living things, than they are to bacteria.

EUKARYOTES

Eukaryotes include all the complex, many-celled organisms of the world—all the plants, animals, fungi, and algae. Eukaryotes also include microbes such as yeasts that help produce wine, beer, and bread. All eukaryotic cells share the same basic architecture.

Eukaryotic cells contain a nucleus, a command center packed with DNA and surrounded by a membrane. They also contain other membrane-bound compartments that carry out specialized tasks. These compartments include bean-shaped mitochondria, which provide the cell with energy.

Some of the microbes that live on your body are eukaryotes. One important group is the fungi. Although not present in huge numbers, microscopic fungi are a part of the microbial community in your gut and on your skin. A few can cause diseases, including skin diseases such as athlete's foot, ringworm, and thrush.

VIRUSES

Viruses are also part of your microbiome. Viruses are able to live and multiply only inside other cells, called host cells, and for that reason, viruses are not considered to be truly alive.

REDRAWING THE TREE OF LIFE

In 1859 British naturalist Charles Darwin published *On the Origin of Species by Means of Natural Selection.* In the book, Darwin presented evidence that all life on Earth is related, descended from a common ancestor. Over a long time, Darwin said, species evolve into different forms, creating great species diversity. Darwin called this connection of all species the tree of life. For more than one hundred years after Darwin, scientists looked at physical features to describe how plants and animals were related on the tree of life. They realized that organisms that looked and behaved alike, such as foxes and wolves, often were closely related. Similarly, microbiologists compared microbes based on their appearance, what they ate, and other obvious features.

By the 1970s, scientists had decided that all life could be grouped into two domains. The first group was the prokaryotes (bacteria). The name comes from the ancient Greek words *pro*, meaning "before," and *karyon*, meaning "nut" or "kernel"—a reference to the nucleus, or kernel, of a cell. In other words, prokaryotes emerged before cells with nuclei. The second group was the eukaryotes (which includes algae, fungi, plants, and animals). The word *eukaryote* contains the ancient Greek prefix *eu*, which means "good" or "well," because eukaryotes have a proper nucleus.

In 1977 Carl Woese, a microbiologist at the University of Illinois, compared microbes in a new way. Instead of describing what microbes looked like or what they ate, he and his coworkers studied a molecule central to the function of the cell, ribosomal ribonucleic acid (RNA), found in cellular structures called ribosomes. Using ribosomal RNA, Woese could more accurately study relationships among bacteria. He could also see clear differences between bacteria and eukaryotes. But when Woese studied the ribosomal RNA of a group of bacteria that made methane, he made a startling discovery: they weren't bacteria at all. They looked like bacteria, but their genes were very different. These microbes weren't closely related to bacteria or eukaryotes. Woese determined that these organisms belonged to a third type of life, which he called the archaea (from an ancient Greek word meaning "primitive" or "original"). Because of Woese's work, most scientists agree that life falls into three domains: bacteria, archaea, and eukaryota.

Viruses are tiny compared to most other microbes. The rhinoviruses—the cause of the common cold—are so small that ten billion of them could fit on the head of a pin. By contrast, only about nine million bacteria would fit on the head of that same pin.

Viruses are made of genetic material packed into a protective protein coat called a capsid. Some viruses have spiky coats surrounding the capsid. Viruses use either DNA or ribonucleic acid (RNA, which is similar in structure to DNA) as their genetic material.

Viruses are very good at one thing: making more of themselves. They latch onto host cells and insert their genetic material. Once the genetic material is inside, the host cell copies this material. Some viruses lie low in the host cell without killing the cell, at least not right away. Other viruses leave the host cell by bursting out and killing the cell at the same time. They then go on to infect other cells.

The role of viruses in the microbiome is poorly understood. Most probably do not make us sick. Instead, they infect bacteria and other members of our microbiome. This may be a good thing, helping to keep our microbial communities stable by killing some microbes and helping others thrive.

"VERY PRETTILY A-MOVING"

Until the seventeenth century, people did not know that the world of microbes even existed. The first person to observe this world was Robert Hooke, an English scientist. He built a microscope and observed many aspects of this hidden world—a spot of mold, the foot of a louse, and the walled cells in a thin slice of cork (which comes from the bark of the cork oak tree). He published his observations in 1665 in his book *Micrographia*, which became a best seller.

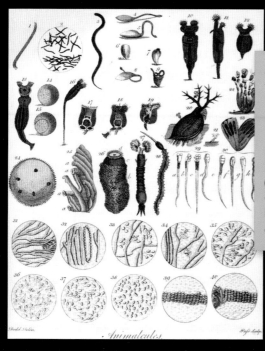

Antoni van Leeuwenhoek first observed "animalcules" under a microscope in the 1670s. In 1796 a London publisher produced a series of hand-colored engravings *(left)* of these microscopic creatures, with artwork based on Leeuwenhoek's original drawings.

A copy of *Micrographia* found its way into the hands of Antoni van Leeuwenhoek, a young fabric merchant living in the Netherlands. Leeuwenhoek was inspired to build microscopes to inspect the quality of cloth. He spent hours and hours grinding glass lenses. Leeuwenhoek's microscopes were more powerful than others available at the time, with a magnifying power of 270x (270 times) or more, and he saw things that no one else had ever seen.

Leeuwenhoek was the first person to observe and study bacteria. In 1676, while trying to discover why spices tasted strong, he stared through a microscope at a drop of water with black pepper in it. He observed very small organisms swimming in the pepper water. He called them animalcules, meaning "little animals." A few years later, Leeuwenhoek became the first person to study the microbes of the human body when he scraped some plaque off his own tooth and viewed it with one of his microscopes. "There were many very little animalcules, very prettily a-moving," he wrote.

Leeuwenhoek then looked at microbes from other mouths. He scraped plaque from the teeth of two women, an eight-year-old

TASTY MICROBES

Fermentation is a process by which microbes break down organic substances, changing their chemical makeup. Food manufacturers often use fermentation to preserve foods, change their form, or enhance their flavors. Cheese is a good example of a food made by fermentation. Milk spoils quickly, but when it is fermented into cheese, it lasts longer, tastes different, and takes the form of a solid rather than a liquid. During fermentation, bacteria from the air convert the lactose (a kind of sugar) in milk to lactic acid, changing the milk's flavor and solidifying it into cheese. As the cheese ferments further, the bacteria convert more and more lactose into lactic acid. The taste becomes stronger and sharper.

Long before humans knew that microbes existed, cooks were using fermentation. Early civilizations, including the ancient Sumerians, Chinese, and Egyptians, fermented fruits, plants, and grain to make alcoholic beverages. The ancient Egyptians used yeast to ferment dough to make bread. Other fermented foods include yogurt, pickles, and soy sauce.

Yeasts are fungi used in fermentation. For instance, yeast can be used to ferment grain to make beer. Many ancient cultures used the process. This model of a brewer making beer was found in the tomb of Meketre, an Egyptian official who lived around 2000 BCE.

child, and a man whose teeth were "all coated over" and who had "never washed his mouth in his whole life." In specimens from all of these people, he found the same tiny creatures, swimming, leaping, and tumbling. Leeuwenhoek regarded these tiny creatures of the body as harmless curiosities. He did not make the connection that something so tiny could dramatically impact a person's health.

THE GERM THEORY OF DISEASE

For a long time after Hooke's and Leeuwenhoek's discoveries, the world of microbes remained on the fringes of science. That changed in the nineteenth century when French chemist Louis Pasteur and German physician Robert Koch connected microbes with disease. At that time, most people believed that disease was caused by miasma, or poisonous air. Pasteur promoted the germ theory of disease, the idea that microbes were responsible for many diseases. Koch demonstrated that specific microbes in the body caused deadly diseases such as tuberculosis, anthrax, and cholera. As proof, Koch extracted microbes from diseased animals, grew the microbes in a laboratory, and injected them into healthy mice. The mice grew sick with the same diseases.

The new way of thinking about disease revolutionized medicine. Doctors and scientists identified disease-causing germs and developed lifesaving treatments, such as a drug to treat syphilis, a sexually transmitted disease caused by a bacterium. People learned how germs spread from person to person—via sneezing, coughing, and unwashed hands, for instance. In the United States and Europe, health officials put a new emphasis on sanitation, personal hygiene, and cleanliness in the home as a way to fight disease.

Although Pasteur promoted germ theory, he did not believe that all microbes were harmful. He thought that the microbes that live in our bodies were good for us, even essential for life. We had evolved to depend on them, Pasteur thought, just as they had evolved to depend on us. But this idea—that microbes could be good for us, even essential—slipped quietly into the background as germ theory came to dominate medical thinking. Health-care workers and the public embraced the idea that all microbes were harmful germs. People tried to rid themselves and their environment of microbes. Beginning in the early twentieth century, Americans diligently scrubbed their bodies; sterilized their homes; and turned up their noses at anything sticky, dirty, or slimy. They didn't realize that in trying to banish germs from their lives, they might have been doing more harm than good.

3

THE GOLDEN ERA OF ANTIBIOTICS

In March 1942, thirty-one-year-old Anne Miller lay dying in a hospital in Connecticut. Miller was suffering from blood poisoning: deadly *Streptococcus* bacteria had invaded her blood. She had developed the infection following a miscarriage about a month before. Miller was delirious and hadn't eaten for weeks. Her temperature kept spiking to over 106°F (41°C). Her doctors had tried surgery, blood transfusions, and newly developed sulfa drugs. All had failed.

The doctors had heard about penicillin, a new, experimental drug that they thought might help. The drug was not yet available for sale to doctors and hospitals, but one of Miller's doctors arranged for some of it to be delivered to his dying patient. About 1 teaspoon (5 ml) of penicillin—half the entire amount in the United States at the time—was rushed by airplane and driven by a state trooper to the hospital where Miller lay dying.

Medical staff injected the experimental drug into Miller's veins every four hours. The next day, her temperature was back to normal for the first time in a month. She sat up in bed and ate heartily, the first time in weeks. A month later, she went home, fully recovered. The new medicine was in such short supply that doctors saved Miller's urine, which contained small amounts of the drug. They extracted penicillin from her urine so the drug could be used in another patient.

Miller lived a long life and died in 1999 at the age of ninety. She was not the first patient to be treated with penicillin. The drug had been tried on a few patients in Oxford, England. But she was the first person to have been saved from death by the new miracle drug.

BACTERIA KILLER

Until the mid-twentieth century, infectious diseases—diseases caused by microbes—were major killers. Mothers routinely died from infections following childbirth. Millions of children succumbed to bacterial diseases such as diphtheria and pneumonia. A child's sore throat could turn into life-threatening scarlet fever. A scratch from a rosebush could become infected with deadly bacteria. Sometimes the only remedy for an infected wound on an arm or leg was amputation of the limb. In World War I (1914–1918), most soldiers died not from guns or bombs but from the infections that settled in after battle wounds.

By the early twentieth century, germ theory had led to a better understanding of the causes of disease. It did not, however, shed much light on how to treat infectious diseases. Doctors and scientists searched for ways to kill bacteria, the cause of many infectious diseases, without harming the patient. But this did not prove to be easy.

Scottish scientist Alexander Fleming, working in a tiny laboratory at Saint Mary's Hospital in London, England, made a

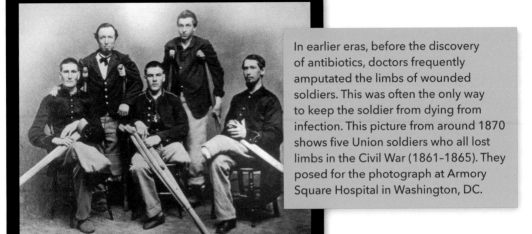

In earlier eras, before the discovery of antibiotics, doctors frequently amputated the limbs of wounded soldiers. This was often the only way to keep the soldier from dying from infection. This picture from around 1870 shows five Union soldiers who all lost limbs in the Civil War (1861–1865). They posed for the photograph at Armory Square Hospital in Washington, DC.

momentous discovery. Fleming was looking for a "wonder drug," a substance that could kill bacteria and be used to fight infections. In his lab in 1928, Fleming was examining petri plates—round, covered dishes filled with a jellylike substance called agar and used for growing microbes. The plates contained colonies of *Staphylococcus*, or staph, bacteria that can cause sore throats, boils, and blood poisoning. On one plate, a patch of fuzzy, greenish mold was growing alongside the staph. The mold was *Penicillium*, which grows on old bread and rotting fruit. The presence of the mold was not unusual. Fleming sometimes took the lids off his petri plates to look at them more closely, and in this case, a stray mold spore from the air must have dropped in. But something else was odd: surrounding the mold was a zone in which all the staph bacteria were dead. Fleming knew what this meant: the mold was killing the bacteria.

The idea of mold as a disease fighter was nothing new. For centuries people had used yeast, bread mold, and mushrooms as treatments for infection. Louis Pasteur and Robert Koch had realized that microbes could kill other microbes. Microbes live in a dog-eat-dog world, and they fight one another to survive. In this struggle for survival, some microbes produce toxic substances that kill off their neighbors. Scientists and doctors call these substances antibiotics, meaning "against life."

Fleming realized that the *Penicillium* on his petri plate contained an antibiotic. Could this be the wonder drug he was seeking? Fleming and his coworkers experimented further. They discovered that the substance not only killed staph, but it also worked against the pathogens that cause pneumonia, gonorrhea, meningitis, and diphtheria. Fleming mixed the mold with a nutrient broth (a liquid used for growing microorganisms) and called the mixture mold juice. He later renamed it penicillin.

Fleming tried to turn penicillin into something medically useful. He tested it in rabbits and mice and found that it was not toxic to the animals. He tried to purify it—that is, to separate the antibacterial agent from the other components of the broth—but the antibacterial property would vanish when he did so. That

In 1928 Scottish scientist Alexander Fleming discovered that *Penicillium*, a genus of mold, worked as an antibiotic. Other scientists furthered his work, ushering in the modern era of antibiotics. Here Fleming is shown in his laboratory at Saint Mary's Hospital in London in 1943.

meant the penicillin was breaking down, decomposing into simpler substances.

Fleming published a paper about his findings in the *British Journal of Experimental Pathology* in 1929. He briefly mentioned how penicillin someday could be used as an antibiotic to treat wounds. But the medical world did not grasp the importance of penicillin. Doctors did not realize that it could be a drug for treating a wide range of infections.

Fleming continued to study penicillin, but he kept hitting the same dead end: the drug quickly lost its antibacterial power when mixed with the nutrient broth. Soon he turned his attention to other pursuits, including new antibacterial chemicals called sulfa drugs. These synthetic (human-made) drugs could be used to treat bacterial infection, but they caused serious side effects, including rashes, vomiting, and kidney damage.

MOLD IN THEIR COATS

More than a decade after Fleming's discovery, penicillin resurfaced in a big way. In 1939 a team led by Howard Florey at Oxford University in England revisited penicillin. With the outbreak of World War II (1939–1945), Great Britain, the United States, the Soviet Union, and partner nations (called the Allies) fought Germany, Japan, Italy, and their partners (called the Axis). On the battlefield, the need for antibacterial drugs was urgent. The Oxford group, like Fleming before them, searched for a substance that could be used to treat infection.

Florey's group picked up where Fleming had left off. They obtained some *Penicillium notatum*, the strain of mold that produces penicillin. Ernst Chain, a Jewish biochemist who had fled Germany to escape the persecution of Jews there, figured out how to purify and concentrate penicillin without it breaking down and losing its power.

The group tested penicillin's antibacterial power in mice. They injected fifty mice with *Streptococcus haemolyticus*, deadly bacteria that in humans cause a variety of dangerous infections. Half of the fifty mice were also injected with penicillin. The other half of the mice got no penicillin. The results were dramatic. The control mice—those not injected with penicillin—all died within sixteen hours. But the penicillin-treated mice behaved normally— they cleaned themselves, ate, and scurried about their cages. Ten days later, the treated mice were still alive and well.

Scientists wondered whether penicillin would work as well in people. Large quantities of penicillin would be needed to test it on humans, so Norman Heatley, another member of the Oxford team, worked at growing large quantities of *Penicillium*. Because Great Britain was at war, laboratory materials were scarce. He took frequent trips to the local dump to look for containers for growing mold, including pie pans, gas cans, cracker tins, and porcelain bedpans.

The group worked under the continual threat of destruction, as German warplanes carried out daily bombing raids on British towns and cities. On breaks between experiments, the scientists dug air-raid shelters and filled sandbags, which were piled up to protect the walls of laboratory buildings from bombs. Worried about losing the penicillin-producing strain of *Penicillium notatum* if they had to flee, the researchers rubbed spores of the mold into their coats. The scientists knew that the mold spores could lie dormant there for years.

THE AGE OF ANTIBIOTICS

In early 1941, the research group—Florey, Heatley, Chain, and others—was ready to try the drug on humans for the first time. They tested it first in Elva Akers, an Oxford woman who was dying of cancer and had only a short time to live. She was proud

PENICILLIN GIRLS

A team of six young women, some as young as sixteen or seventeen, played an indispensable part in the development of penicillin during World War II. In the research labs in Oxford, England, these "penicillin girls" *(left)* worked to grow and harvest the *Penicillium* mold. They washed and sterilized vessels scrounged from local dumps, filled them with nutrient broth, and spiked the broth with mold spores. After the mold had grown, the young women suctioned off the mold-infused fluid for experiments. They worked six days a week, often long hours, and occasionally on Sundays. They earned one British pound a week, equal to about four dollars. The young women were aware of the importance of their work. They knew that success could benefit wounded soldiers and other sick people.

to help learn if penicillin was safe for humans. It was. Then the research group tested it on an Oxford police officer, Albert Alexander, who was suffering from a raging infection from a rosebush scratch on his face. The drug calmed the infection, and Alexander began to recover. But supplies of penicillin were very limited, and without enough of the drug to kill all the bacteria, Alexander relapsed and died.

In mid-1941, Florey and Heatley traveled to the United States to persuade US drug companies to produce penicillin. They set up shop in a US Department of Agriculture laboratory in Peoria, Illinois. One challenge they faced was that Fleming's original mold did not produce much penicillin. To find a mold that produced more, the scientists asked everyone they knew in Peoria for samples of soil, moldy grain, fruits, and vegetables. An assistant, Mary Hunt—nicknamed Moldy Mary—scoured local markets for moldy cheese and rotting fruit. On one trip, Hunt brought back a moldy cantaloupe. The *Penicillium* that grew on this cantaloupe was so powerful that scientists used it as a parent strain to produce more penicillin. To this day, most of the penicillin produced in the world comes from this strain.

As more of the drug became available, doctors gave it to other patients—including Anne Miller—and it helped them recover from infections that would otherwise have been deadly. By 1942 the value of penicillin to the war effort was obvious. In 1943 the US War Production Board (WPB), an agency that oversaw the production

Indiana-based Schenley Laboratories was one of twenty-one US companies authorized to produce penicillin during World War II. The company promoted the lifesaving drug in this wartime advertisement.

and distribution of materials needed by the US military, took control of penicillin production in the United States. The WPB chose twenty-one US companies to manufacture penicillin on a large scale. In 1943 Allied doctors began treating soldiers with the drug, curing thousands of wound infections on the battlefield. In 1944 the US government approved the sale of the drug to the American public. British authorities approved it the following year. In 1945 the Nobel Committee awarded Fleming, Florey, and Chain the Nobel Prize in Medicine for their work on penicillin. The Nobel Prize is given each year to those who make important contributions for the good of humanity in a variety of disciplines.

Discoveries of other antibiotics soon followed. In 1944 Albert Schatz and Selman Waksman, microbiologists at Rutgers University in New Jersey, discovered streptomycin, an antibiotic made by soil bacteria. Then came the discovery of tetracycline, erythromycin, chloramphenicol, and isoniazid. Before long, scientists had examined a whole spectrum of antibiotics in clinical trials (tests done on human participants). In the United States, the US Food and Drug Administration (FDA) approved these medicines for treating a wide range of bacterial infections.

These discoveries launched a golden era in medicine: the age of antibiotics. Doctors finally had a powerful way to treat infection. Diseases that had once been debilitating or deadly to millions of people around the globe—diseases such as meningitis, childbirth fever, pneumonia, scarlet fever, gonorrhea, syphilis, and tuberculosis—could now be cured.

THE AGE OF MIRACLES
The discovery of penicillin marked a turning point in medicine. Many doctors, manufacturers, and patients came to regard antibiotics as magical cure-alls. For this reason, and to earn profits from the new miracle drugs, manufacturers put penicillin

HOW ANTIBIOTICS WORK

Antibiotics are powerful drugs that doctors use for treating infection because the medicines kill bacteria without harming the body. Antibiotics work by targeting structures or chemical processes that bacterial cells have but that human cells don't. Penicillin, for example, stops many kinds of bacteria from building cell walls. Because human cells don't have cell walls, the drug has no effect on them.

Antibiotics are grouped into the following five different classes, according to how they work:

1. They block construction of the bacterial cell wall. The cell wall grows thinner, and the cell bursts and dies.
2. They block protein formation in the bacterial cells. Proteins are vital for life, and without them, a cell can't survive.
3. They stop bacteria from dividing and growing by blocking the replication, or reproduction, of DNA.
4. They prevent bacteria from producing vitamins they need to grow.
5. They punch holes in bacteria cell membranes, causing the cell contents to leak out and killing the cell.

into a wide variety of everyday products such as mouthwash, cough drops, soap, and first-aid lotion. Until the mid-1950s, US consumers could buy penicillin at drugstores without a prescription. People sometimes took it for minor illnesses such as sore throats and runny noses. But these illnesses are usually caused by viruses, not bacteria, so the antibiotics did no good.

The misuse of penicillin and other antibiotics by patients and doctors in the mid-twentieth century caused the drugs to lose their power. That's because giving antibiotics in weak doses or taking them for too short a duration often kills most but not all the bacteria infecting a patient. The bacteria that survive are

Crowds Spread THROAT INFECTION

for RELIEF and PROTECTION from SORE THROAT TONSILLITIS LARYNGITIS HOARSENESS COUGHS COLDS CATARRH

Suck MAC *Antiseptic* THROAT SWEETS
BRAND

This British advertisement from the 1950s or early 1960s promotes throat lozenges containing amylmetacresol, an antibacterial substance similar to antibiotics. In the twenty-first century, manufacturers still add antibacterial chemicals to soaps, hand sanitizers, toothpaste, cosmetics, and other consumer products. These chemicals can contribute to the growth of drug-resistant bacteria.

those with a genetic mutation, or variation, that makes them able to resist the antibiotic. These resistant bacteria reproduce, move on to infect other people, and resist even stronger doses of antibiotics. Over time, the number of drug-resistant bacteria increases, challenging the medical profession to find new drugs to treat common illnesses.

By the 1950s, hospitals were reporting alarming cases where antibiotics had failed to stop infections. Alexander Fleming had warned that this could happen. In his Nobel Prize acceptance speech in 1945, he had predicted that the misuse of penicillin could help breed mutant forms of bacteria that could resist the drug. "It is not difficult to make microbes resistant to penicillin in the laboratory by exposing them to concentrations not sufficient to kill them, and the same thing has occasionally happened in the body," Fleming said. Resistant bacteria called the future of the golden age of antibiotics into question.

4

"SWALLOWING A GRENADE": THE ANTIBIOTIC PROBLEM

Since the 1940s, antibiotics have given doctors a powerful way to destroy bacteria that make humans sick. In the twentieth century, however, bacteria evolved to resist all the major classes of antibiotics. The rise of antibiotic-resistant bacteria has weakened these once-powerful drugs, and they are losing their punch. The misuse of antibiotics has helped create antibiotic-resistant "superbugs," bacteria that have developed resistance to a number of antibiotics and that are untreatable. Once again, bacteria are becoming deadly killers.

In the twenty-first century, according to the US Centers for Disease Control and Prevention (CDC), antibiotic-resistant bacteria kill about twenty-three thousand Americans every year. The rise of resistance is a serious health problem worldwide as well. A project called Review on Antimicrobial Resistance, sponsored

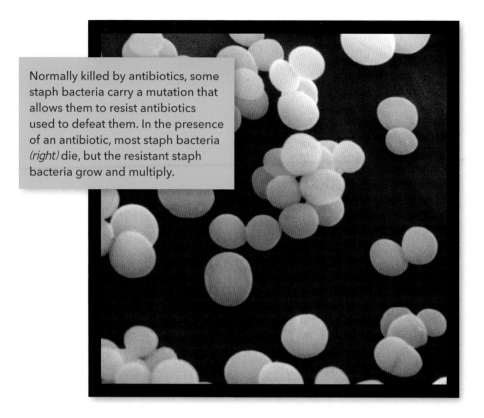

Normally killed by antibiotics, some staph bacteria carry a mutation that allows them to resist antibiotics used to defeat them. In the presence of an antibiotic, most staph bacteria *(right)* die, but the resistant staph bacteria grow and multiply.

by the United Kingdom, estimates that worldwide, antibiotic resistance causes seven hundred thousand deaths per year.

THE EVOLUTION OF RESISTANCE

Imagine a woman who develops a skin infection. A population of *Staphylococcus aureus* is growing out of control on her skin, producing a painful rash. Her doctor prescribes an antibiotic cream, and the woman rubs the cream into her skin.

The antibiotic in the lotion kills most of the *S. aureus*. So far, so good. The antibiotic worked—mostly. But the *S. aureus* microbes on her skin aren't all identical. Some may carry mutations in their DNA that make them different from the others. Some of the mutated *S. aureus* bacteria might be resistant to the drug. "You have many millions of bacteria," explains University

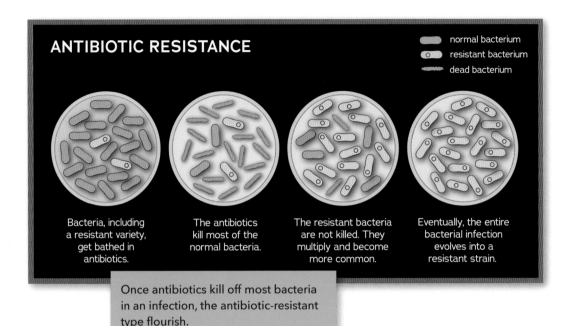

ANTIBIOTIC RESISTANCE

- normal bacterium
- resistant bacterium
- dead bacterium

Bacteria, including a resistant variety, get bathed in antibiotics.

The antibiotics kill most of the normal bacteria.

The resistant bacteria are not killed. They multiply and become more common.

Eventually, the entire bacterial infection evolves into a resistant strain.

Once antibiotics kill off most bacteria in an infection, the antibiotic-resistant type flourish.

of Minnesota biologist Marlene Zuk. "So it's not too surprising that they vary, the way a big city will tend to have at least a few people with unusual eye color, exceptionally small feet or any other characteristic."

How exactly do bacteria resist an antibiotic? Scientists have discovered that some bacteria can disable the antibiotic by chemically changing it. Bacteria can also change in ways that make them resistant to the antibiotic. They may close up gates in the plasma membrane that normally allow an antibiotic to enter a cell or may pump the antibiotic out of the cell before it can do any harm.

After antibiotic treatment, the resistant bacteria do what all bacteria do: they multiply. Because the antibiotic has killed off all susceptible bacteria, the resistant bacteria can multiply without competition to check their growth. In other words, before the antibiotic, only a few bacteria carried the resistance gene. After the antibiotic, many more bacteria have the resistance gene.

This is a form of Darwin's idea of natural selection, or survival of the fittest. By changing the environment in which bacteria live and grow—through the introduction of an antibiotic—humans can create conditions in which resistant bacteria are actually more likely to survive and reproduce.

Not all bacteria that develop resistance are pathogens, however. Resistance may also evolve among mutualists or commensals, the beneficial or harmless members of the human microbiome. But any antibiotic-resistant bacteria, even beneficial ones, can be dangerous because the resistance can spread to harmful bacteria.

THE SPREAD OF RESISTANCE

Bacteria are fast evolvers. They reproduce quickly and are always present in huge numbers, which speeds the rate of evolution. As resistant bacteria grow and multiply, they pass down resistance genes to their many offspring. In response to abundant use of antibiotics, bacteria evolve resistance very quickly. As a result, if antibiotics are overused, they can quickly become ineffective.

Some bacteria have a genetic quirk that allows resistance to spread even faster than usual: they swap genes with one another. This process is called horizontal gene transfer. Here's how it works: Bacterial genes can be present on the bacterial chromosome as well as on plasmids (small, circular pieces of DNA inside bacteria). Bacteria can pass plasmids back and forth to one another. Bacteria can also incorporate plasmid DNA into their chromosomes, which allows the bacteria to pass the DNA to their offspring when they replicate. This swapping of plasmid DNA can take place between identical and distantly related species, and the swapping speeds the rate at which bacteria evolve resistance to antibiotics. If a plasmid transfers a resistance gene to a helpful species of bacteria, those bacteria

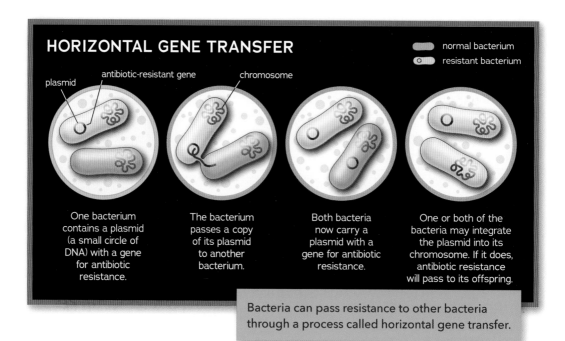

HORIZONTAL GENE TRANSFER

normal bacterium

resistant bacterium

plasmid

antibiotic-resistant gene

chromosome

One bacterium contains a plasmid (a small circle of DNA) with a gene for antibiotic resistance.

The bacterium passes a copy of its plasmid to another bacterium.

Both bacteria now carry a plasmid with a gene for antibiotic resistance.

One or both of the bacteria may integrate the plasmid into its chromosome. If it does, antibiotic resistance will pass to its offspring.

Bacteria can pass resistance to other bacteria through a process called horizontal gene transfer.

can in turn pass the gene to a harmful species of bacteria, creating a drug-resistant pathogen.

Sometimes plasmids carry multiple resistance genes, which can give rise to dangerous types of bacteria known as superbugs. Superbugs, also called multi-drug-resistant bacteria, are resistant to more than one type of antibiotic. Superbugs are dangerous because they are very difficult—sometimes impossible—to treat using available antibiotics.

In the twenty-first century, as resistance spreads and superbugs develop, bacteria that were once curable are becoming dangerous again. A good example is gonococcus, a bacterium that causes the sexually transmitted disease gonorrhea. Gonococcus is resistant to three types of antibiotics. Some strains of gonococcus are resistant to a fourth type of antibiotic. Because of this resistance, doctors are losing their ability to treat gonorrhea. If left untreated, it can lead to infertility and even death.

Hospitals, where patients routinely take antibiotics, are an ideal place for antibiotic resistance to develop. Some hospital patients receive antibiotics to treat infections. Others receive antibiotics to prevent infection during surgery. Yet this abundant use of antibiotics creates an ideal breeding ground for resistant bacteria. Once resistant bacteria evolve, they don't stay put. In hospitals, family members come to visit patients, bringing cards and flowers. They hug or touch patients, and through this physical contact, they may leave the facility with resistant bacteria clinging to their hands. These bacteria can pass from person to person just about anywhere, through coughing, sneezing, or touching doorknobs with unwashed hands. Bacteria can spread throughout a school, workplace, or day-care center. They can ride inside a bus or car or hop on a plane and fly around the world.

HAND HYGIENE

Washing your hands is one of the most effective ways to prevent bacterial infection. When you wash, use plain soap and water and follow these steps:

1. Wet your hands with clean, running water (warm or cold). Turn off the tap and apply soap.
2. Lather your hands by rubbing them together with the soap. Don't forget to lather the backs of your hands, between your fingers, and under your nails.
3. Scrub for at least twenty seconds. That is about as long as it takes to hum "Happy Birthday to You" from beginning to end twice.
4. Rinse your hands well under clean, running water.
5. Dry your hands with a clean towel or air-dry them.

MRSA

The most well-known superbug and one of the most frightening is methicillin-resistant *Staphylococcus aureus* (MRSA). This pathogen can cause wound infections, pneumonia, and bloodstream infections.

Normally, *S. aureus* lives on human skin along with other members of the human microbiome and eats oil and dead skin cells to help ward off pathogens. But if *S. aureus* gets into the human body—either through a small cut or scrape or through a large wound such as the kind created during surgery—the bacteria can cause a serious infection.

In the 1940s, doctors could effectively treat *S. aureus* with penicillin. By the 1950s, strains resistant to penicillin had become common. In 1960 doctors began to treat *S. aureus* with a new drug, methicillin, a laboratory-made antibiotic. Doctors thought it would be effective against *S. aureus* for decades. But within one year, doctors began to encounter strains that were resistant to methicillin.

How did this happen? The *S. aureus* that lives on someone's skin is exposed to antibiotics when that person takes an antibiotic to treat a different kind of bacteria. *S. aureus* can then pick up resistance genes from other members of the microbiome through horizontal gene transfer. This is how *S. aureus* picked up a gene for vancomycin resistance in the late 1990s. Vancomycin is a powerful antibiotic, a last-ditch drug that doctors turn to when other antibiotics fail to stop an infection. Scientists discovered that MRSA had picked up the gene for vancomycin resistance by horizontal gene transfer from resistant *Enterococcus faecalis*, a normal resident of the human gut.

In the twenty-first century, doctors routinely encounter strains of MRSA that resist a long list of antibiotics. One study showed that plasmids found in MRSA carry genes for resistance to the antibiotic penicillin, streptomycin, vancomycin, and trimethoprim

A researcher holds a petri plate containing a strain of bacteria called methicillin-resistant *Staphylococcus aureus* (MRSA). Although MRSA was named for its methicillin resistance, it is also resistant to many other types of antibiotics. Each year, more than eleven thousand Americans die from MRSA infections.

and to a disinfectant found in many brands of wet wipes. *S. aureus* is the most common cause of infection in hospital patients, causing five hundred thousand serious illnesses a year. MRSA has also shown up in schoolchildren, football players, prisoners, survivors of Hurricane Katrina (which hit New Orleans, Louisiana, in 2005), and recipients of tattoos created with unsterilized equipment. In 2011 the CDC reported more than eleven thousand deaths and eighty thousand serious MRSA infections nationwide.

INNOCENT BYSTANDERS

Antibiotics are some of the most commonly prescribed drugs in the world. But doctors often prescribe them unnecessarily, or too often. For example, the typical American child has received three courses of antibiotics by aged two, ten courses by aged ten, and seventeen courses by the time he or she reaches adulthood. By aged forty, the average American has taken thirty courses of antibiotics. Antibiotics are necessary for treating serious bacterial infections and can be lifesaving in some cases, but many experts say that our use of them is simply too high. What's more, antibiotics aren't used only to treat sick people. They are also added to some soaps, body washes, and cosmetics, to give users the feeling they are gaining protection against bacteria.

The overuse of antibiotics has not only fueled the rise of resistant bacteria. It has also had an impact on beneficial bacteria. Antibiotics don't just kill pathogens. They kill resident helpful microbes as well. "When we take a pill of vancomycin, it's like swallowing a grenade," writes science journalist Carl Zimmer. "It may kill our enemy, but it kills a lot of bystanders, too."

Antibiotics change the balance of microbes in our bodies, and that can make us more susceptible to infections. For instance, yeast infections, which can occur in the mouth, on the feet, or on the genitals, are a common side effect of antibiotic treatment. A yeast infection happens when an antibiotic kills off beneficial microbes that normally keep populations of the fungus *Candida* in check. With the helper microbes gone, *Candida* grows out of control.

Another normally harmless species of bacteria is *Clostridium difficile*, also known as *C. diff*. In a healthy person, *C. diff* is just one of the trillions of bacteria species that reside in the gut. But when strong antibiotics wipe out the normal gut microbiome, *C. diff* can take over. The bug eats away at the lining of the gut and causes horrible, debilitating diarrhea. Almost 250,000 Americans each year require hospital care for *C. diff*, and at least fourteen thousand people die as a result of the infection. In most of these cases, the use of antibiotics is a major factor contributing to the illness. What's more, the main treatment for *C. diff* infection is additional antibiotics. Yet strains of *C. diff* have been evolving antibiotic resistance, which can render these antibiotics useless.

ON THE FARM

Antibiotics are some of the most commonly prescribed drugs in the world. In 2010 doctors prescribed 258 million courses of antibiotics to patients in the United States. Yet most antibiotics aren't given to people. More than half of all antibiotics administered in the United States are used on farm animals.

In the 1940s, scientists discovered that giving animals low doses of antibiotics made them grow faster. Chicks given antibiotics grew faster and fatter than chicks that received no antibiotics. Piglets given antibiotics in their food grew fatter than those who received antibiotic-free food. Soon farmers across the United States were feeding low doses of antibiotics to cows, pigs, chickens, turkeys, and other livestock animals. In the twenty-first century, some antibiotics on farms are used to treat sick animals, but this represents only a small fraction of total antibiotic use. Many more antibiotics are given to healthy animals as a way to promote growth or to prevent animals kept in crowded and unsanitary conditions from getting sick. In 2013 US farmers fed roughly 32.6 million pounds (14.8 million kg) of antibiotics to livestock animals, up from 30 million pounds (13.6 million kg) in 2011.

Dosing animals with antibiotics may seem like a good idea. After all, by promoting quick growth, the practice allows farmers to bring more products to market more quickly, thereby increasing profits for farmers while also bringing down the cost of meat and other farm products for consumers. But the steady diet of antibiotics fed to farm animals breeds bacteria that are resistant to antibiotics, just as it does with overuse in humans.

Additionally, in just a few small steps, antibiotics and resistant bacteria can pass from farms to people. For example, antibiotics that are fed to animals exit their bodies through urine. At animal feedlots—facilities where cattle and other livestock animals are fattened before slaughter—urine and other liquid waste, which is often laced with antibiotic residue, can seep into nearby waterways and groundwater. People draw their drinking water from these sources and thereby ingest the antibiotics. (Water treatment plants, which process water for drinking, don't remove antibiotics from the water.)

Antibiotic-resistant bacteria can also arrive in our kitchens on meat and poultry and inside eggs. If the meat or eggs

Industrial farms routinely give antibiotics to livestock. For reasons not yet understood, antibiotics promote weight gain, so farmers primarily use them to quickly fatten animals for slaughter. The widespread use of antibiotics on farms has contributed to the emergence of antibiotic-resistant bacteria in both humans and animals.

are properly cooked, the bacteria are killed. But if they are undercooked, people can eat the still-living bacteria. If a cook doesn't thoroughly wash a knife or cutting board on which raw meat or eggs have been handled and then uses that same equipment to prepare a salad or other dish, everyone who eats the salad might also ingest the resistant bacteria.

Eating food contaminated with bacteria or other microbes can cause food poisoning. In a rising number of cases, the bacteria that cause food poisoning are antibiotic-resistant, making food poisoning much more difficult to treat. Two common food-borne bacteria—*Campylobacter* and *Salmonella*—send 3 to 4 million Americans to the doctor or hospital every year. Of those cases, about 440,000 per year are caused by antibiotic-resistant strains of *Campylobacter* and *Salmonella*.

In the United States, researchers and health advocates have argued strongly against the practice of feeding antibiotics to healthy animals. The CDC recommends phasing out the practice, as does the American Medical Association, the American Public Health Association, and the American Academy of Pediatrics. The CDC stated in a 2013 report, "Up to half of antibiotic use in humans and much of antibiotic use in animals is unnecessary and inappropriate and makes everyone less safe."

The practice of giving antibiotics to healthy animals could be on its way out. In response to pressure from consumers, Perdue Farms, one of the country's largest producers of chickens, announced in 2014 that it was stopping the use of antibiotics for growth promotion in its animals. In 2015 the McDonald's fast-food chain announced that within two years, it would no longer serve chicken raised with antibiotics used in human medicine—the kind that can create resistant bacteria in people—although it will continue to treat chickens with animal-specific antibiotics that aren't used on humans. Under pressure from consumers, other food companies, restaurants, and supermarkets are also phasing out antibiotics or offering antibiotic-free options.

SLOWING ANTIBIOTIC RESISTANCE

The evolution of antibiotic resistance is a serious public health concern. Antibiotics are extremely valuable drugs, and if we use them wisely, we can control antibiotic resistance. Resistance cannot be stopped altogether, however, because bacteria will continue to evolve, but it can be slowed. The CDC recommends several steps for protecting yourself from resistant bacteria.

One is to stay as healthy as possible. You might not be able to avoid all illnesses, but you can protect your health by preparing food safely and washing your hands frequently with soap that does not contain antibacterial ingredients. You can also get vaccinated against common, dangerous diseases. A vaccine, administered by a medical professional, usually through an injection, protects you from a specific disease by introducing a weakened form of the disease into your body. The vaccine triggers your immune system to produce proteins called antibodies, which fight the disease. If you encounter the actual disease after receiving a vaccine, the antibodies will keep you from getting sick. Getting the vaccines recommended by your doctor is a good idea. Not only do vaccines protect you from deadly diseases, they cause these diseases to become less common in the general public. That keeps everyone healthier.

Another CDC recommendation is to use antibiotics wisely. Sometimes patients wanting quick relief from painful or fatiguing symptoms pressure doctors into prescribing antibiotics, whether or not they actually have a bacterial infection. Some doctors may prescribe antibiotics as a precaution, to ward off the remote possibility of an infection. Instead, patients should be very cautious in asking their doctors for antibiotics, and doctors should prescribe antibiotics only when needed to treat serious infections. Patients should also take antibiotics exactly as directed. They should complete the entire course of antibiotics as prescribed, even if they start to feel better right away. If patients stop their antibiotic treatment too soon, they risk killing off only the weak bacteria and allowing the strongest ones to survive and reproduce.

New antibiotics are also desperately needed to keep up with resistant bacteria. Gram-negative bacteria are the most worrisome bacteria because they are becoming resistant to nearly all available antibiotics. However, few new antibiotics are being developed. Even though scientists test thousands of natural and synthetic substances in the search for new antibiotics, they tend to uncover the same already-known antibiotics over and over. When scientists do find a new antibiotic, it can't be sold to the public right away. In the United States, drug companies must win approval from the FDA before putting new drugs on the

SOAP VERSUS ANTIBIOTIC

Soap protects us from bacteria. Antibiotics protect us from bacteria. But bacteria don't become resistant to soap. That's because soap and water simply wash bacteria away rather than killing them. And soap and water don't discriminate. They wash all kinds of bacteria—including helpful bacteria—down the drain.

Antibiotics, on the other hand, kill off susceptible bacteria but not resistant bacteria. With the susceptible bacteria gone, the resistant bacteria multiply and become more common. That's why it matters how you get rid of bacteria. Often it's far more effective to wash away bacteria than to use antibiotics—unless you have a serious, life-threatening illness, infection, or wound. And when you use soap, avoid brands that are labeled "antibacterial"—they contain antibiotics.

ANTIBIOTICS AROUND THE WORLD

Antibiotic overuse is a worldwide problem. Antibiotics are heavily used in wealthy nations that have modern, well-developed health-care systems, such as the United States, Japan, and South Korea. But antibiotic use is also on the rise in some less wealthy countries, including India, Kenya, and Vietnam. When antibiotics are overused in a country, antibiotic resistance also rises there.

A few wealthy European countries, including Denmark and Sweden, have low rates of antibiotic use, which has lowered antibiotic resistance there. In these countries, health organizations teach citizens about the dangers of overusing antibiotics. Dr. Ramanan Laxminarayan, director of the Washington, DC–based Center for Disease Dynamics, Economics and Policy, would like to see more nations adopt such efforts. He says, "In the absence of antibiotics, resistant bacteria more easily die out. In many cases, if we stop overusing antibiotics, resistance will go substantially down."

market. The approval involves lengthy studies and tests of human participants. These can take many years to complete. In total, it can cost around $1 billion to bring a new antibiotic to market. Drug companies might be reluctant to spend this money, because antibiotics aren't very profitable for them. For example, a man may take antibiotics for a week to clear up a skin infection. But if that same man has high blood pressure, he may take drugs to lower his blood pressure for years. Drug companies would prefer to put their research dollars into drugs, such as blood pressure medication, that will give them many years of sales and profits.

What's more, antibiotics lose their usefulness quickly because bacteria quickly evolve to resist them. For instance, the antibiotic linezolid arrived on the market in 2000, and resistance to it arrived in 2001. Daptomycin arrived in 2003, and resistance to it showed up in 2004. Knowing that an antibiotic may be useful for only a short time, a drug company might be unwilling to invest time and money to bring it to market.

With the pressing need for new antibiotics and with drug companies hesitant to develop them, some advocates argue that the US government should take the lead. They want the government to provide more funding for antibiotic research or to offer meaningful tax breaks or other incentives for companies to research and develop new antibiotics.

5
A New Era

ike humans, all animals have their own unique communities of microbes. But could an animal survive without its microbes? Scientists think that's an important question. If we could raise animals without microbes, we could compare them to animals with microbes to see how they differ. This could give researchers clues about the role of microbes in both animal and human health—and what happens when we tinker with them.

Mice without Microbes

In 1945 James Reyniers and his coworkers at the University of Notre Dame in Indiana became the first scientists to raise animals without microbes—so-called germ-free animals. The animal they chose to test was a mouse. Raising germ-free mice was not easy. Researchers had to deliver baby mice surgically so that the newborns wouldn't pick up microbes from the mother's birth canal. To prevent the mice from picking up microbes from the air, researchers had to create a sterile delivery room and sterile, sealed chambers in which the mice would live. Investigators had to perform all experiments without directly touching the mice so as not to pass microbes through physical contact. They wore gloves to reach inside the chambers through external openings. The researchers also ensured that the mice ate only sterilized food, drank only sterilized water, and breathed only sterilized air.

How did Reyniers's germ-free mice fare? They survived, but they showed noticeable differences when compared to mice with microbes. The germ-free mice had swollen bellies because their intestines didn't develop properly. They also required richer food and about 30 percent more calories to gain the same weight as

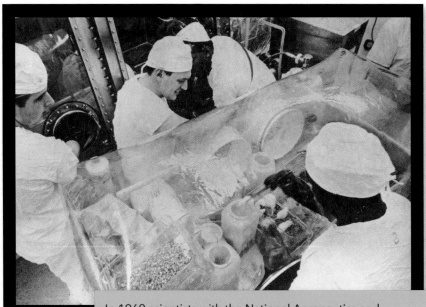

In 1969 scientists with the National Aeronautics and Space Administration (NASA) studied germ-free mice to determine how substances from the moon would affect the microbiomes of living things on Earth.

control mice. In mice, as in people, gut microbes make enzymes that aid in digestion. Without these microbes, the mice couldn't process their food as efficiently, so they needed more of it to grow to a normal, healthy size.

Germ-free mice showed other differences too. They were missing vitamin K, so their blood wouldn't clot on its own, and researchers had to administer the important vitamin to the mice. (Using data about the lack of vitamin K in germ-free mice, later researchers discovered that microbes in the gut are responsible for making vitamin K.)

The mice also had impaired immune systems and were very susceptible to infection. If a germ managed to sneak into a chamber, it quickly led to the animal's death. Without microbes, the mice were unable to fight off infection, so researchers were able to confirm that microbes help the immune system develop and function properly.

The researchers determined that germ-free mice could survive without their microbes, but only with special, carefully controlled diets and by using extreme measures to keep all germs away from them. These experiments gave early clues that in the real world, microbes help mice—and people—survive. They digest complex and varied foods, make vitamins, and help train the immune system to keep out dangerous invaders.

THE LIMITS OF CULTURE

Experiments with germ-free animals gave the first hints about what microbes do, but many questions remained. What types of microbes live in and on humans? How do they interact with our digestive system and our immune system? How are they impacted by antibiotics and other aspects of modern life?

For most of the twentieth century, answering those questions was nearly impossible. It was difficult for scientists to get a clear

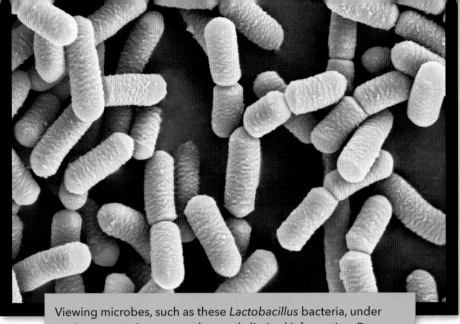

Viewing microbes, such as these *Lactobacillus* bacteria, under a microscope gives researchers only limited information. By studying the DNA of microbes, scientists can learn much more.

picture of the human ecosystem. For one thing, microbes are invisible. Scientists can observe them with a microscope, but even under magnification, many microbes look very similar. In addition, what they look like doesn't tell us much. Often what distinguishes microbes is what they do—what they eat, how they behave, and how they interact with one another.

Scientists can culture, or grow, microbes in the laboratory, in petri plates containing agar. In these laboratory conditions, some kinds of microbes will grow and multiply. A single bacterium can grow into a colony of millions of bacteria within a few days. Scientists can then identify and study these colonies. However, most microbes of the body are so adapted to growing on teeth or behind the ear that they refuse to grow in a laboratory. Microbes that can't be cultured are nearly impossible to study and identify. That is why, for most of the twentieth century, scientists found it impossible to understand which microbes were growing in and on the human body and what they were doing. It wasn't until scientists developed a powerful new way of looking at microbes that they began to understand the vast and complicated ecosystems of our bodies.

A Window on Microbial Diversity

At about the same time antibiotics were changing medicine, in the late twentieth century, a revolution was under way in biology. Over many decades in the twentieth century, teams of biologists discovered that the instructions for making and operating living things are written in DNA. Scientists deciphered the structure of DNA and learned how the genetic code—or the arrangement of chemicals in DNA—directs processes in living cells. Scientists also learned how to read the genetic code. The laboratory technique by which scientists read this code is called DNA sequencing.

In the 1990s, David Relman, a physician at Stanford University in California, used DNA sequencing to study types of human microbes that couldn't be successfully grown in a petri plate. On a routine trip to the dentist, Relman decided to get a sample of the microbes in his mouth. "I went into work first, picked up some sterile collection tubes, brought them with me to the dentist's office, and asked him, as he was cleaning my teeth, would he mind putting this stuff into these tubes, instead of throwing it out," Relman said.

He brought the tubes of his dental microbes back to his lab. Instead of trying to grow the microbes on petri plates, as was the usual scientific protocol, Relman and his colleagues studied the microbial DNA to see what was living in the tubes. They used a technique called polymerase chain reaction (PCR) to copy small amounts of DNA from the sample over and over, creating more DNA. Relman and his team were able to study all the microbes in the sample—even those that wouldn't grow on a petri plate—simply by looking at the sequences of DNA in the sample.

INSIDE DNA

Each DNA molecule is made of two long strands containing chemical compounds called bases. The two strands resemble a twisted rope ladder. The bases form an alphabet, similar to a written alphabet, but with just four letters: *A, G, T,* and *C.* These letters stand for chemical names: *A* stands for adenine, *T* for thymine, *G* for guanine, and *C* for cytosine. The sequence, or arrangement, of the bases in DNA carries instructions for making proteins. Proteins are involved in nearly every process in the human body, from food digestion to the functioning of the immune system. Proteins also make skin, hair, blood, and internal organs.

All living things, including microbes, pass copies of their DNA to their offspring. As a microbe prepares to divide (reproduce), it copies its DNA, carefully replicating the sequence of bases so that its offspring has the exact same DNA and, as a result, the same characteristics as the parent microbe. Sometimes a mistake happens and the bases in DNA are copied incorrectly, producing a mutation. Over time, mutations in DNA can lead to the development of new species.

All living cells—including microbial cells—contain DNA, a substance that directs how cells and organisms grow, function, and reproduce. By examining the arrangement of chemical compounds on strands of DNA *(above)*, scientists can identify microbes and determine how they function. The four chemical compounds, called bases, are adenine (A), thymine (T), guanine (G), and cytosine (C).

TAKING A DNA FINGERPRINT

When investigators want to learn which microbes are present in a sample of bacteria, they focus their attention on the 16S ribosomal RNA (16S rRNA) gene, which codes for (contains instructions for making) an essential part of ribosomes. All prokaryotes have the 16S rRNA gene, but each species has a slightly different version. Researchers can identify a microbe from just its 16S rRNA sequence the same way that police can identify someone from that person's unique fingerprint.

Over time, scientists have uploaded the DNA sequences of tens of thousands of microbes into giant databases. With the 16S rRNA sequence of a specific microbe in hand, scientists can search these databases to help identify microbes. If they find a database match, they have identified a known species of microbe. If they don't find a match, they have uncovered a new species.

This process represented a profound shift in the way scientists studied microbes of the body. Relman had neatly sidestepped the problem of growing bacteria in culture. No longer were scientists limited to studying microbes that grew well in the lab. Instead, the use of DNA sequencing allowed investigators to "see" bacteria that had previously been out of bounds.

Relman and his colleagues discovered that DNA sequencing gave a much broader picture of what was living between his teeth and gums than did culturing. Their results hinted that the human ecosystem was packed with previously unidentified microbes and that the human microbiome was much more diverse than anyone had suspected. The microbes also seemed to be contributing to overall human health. "These are almost entirely all organisms whose presence is not something to fear or be worried about, but rather, something for which to be thankful," says Relman. "To a large degree our microbial inhabitants are contributing to our own health. They are a fundamental part of who we are as healthy . . . adaptable living organisms."

THE MODERN MICROBIOME ERA

DNA sequencing has indeed transformed how researchers study the microbiome. Researchers can perform DNA sequencing on a single microbe's genome—its complete set of DNA—or they can perform DNA sequencing on complex samples full of many microbes. By looking for specific marker genes (genes that identify different species of microbes), researchers can quickly identify all the microbes in the sample.

Advances in sequencing technology have allowed investigators to go a step further and ask, "What are the microbes doing?" To answer this question, researchers sequence the metagenome, the complete genome of every microbe present in any given sample. In metagenomic sequencing, investigators can't tell which genes belong to which microbe. But by looking at all the genes together, they can understand the community of microbes as a whole, such as the entire community of microbes in a person's mouth.

In the years following Relman's pioneering work, DNA sequencing—which was once time-consuming and very expensive—has become fast and cheap. As a result, the understanding of the bugs that colonize the human body has progressed at lightning speed. So has our understanding of how much they contribute to our health.

6

TAKING A
CLOSER LOOK

Much of what scientists know about the human ecosystem comes from the Human Microbiome Project, a five-year project begun in 2007 to assess microbes from different body sites of healthy young US adults. The $157 million project, carried out by the US National Institutes of Health (NIH), aimed to take stock of all the bacteria, archaea, fungi, and viruses that colonize the mouth, gut, armpits, and other parts of the human body. The project involved the participation of more than two hundred researchers from all over the country.

The first challenge was to find healthy Americans to study. The researchers examined 600 adult volunteers between the ages of eighteen and forty. They weighed the volunteers to make sure they were neither too fat nor too thin. Dentists examined the volunteers' gums and teeth. Gynecologists examined the female volunteers for genital yeast infections.

Of the 600 volunteers, many were not completely healthy, and the researchers chose only those 250 volunteers who were in tip-top shape.

Next, the scientists sampled the microbiome from each of these healthy volunteers. They swabbed mouths, noses, and ears. They collected stool samples to examine gut microbes. In all, men were sampled in fifteen body sites, women in eighteen, including three places in the vagina. The extra samples taken from the women enabled scientists to study the role played by vaginal microbes during pregnancy and childbirth.

To determine the identity of the bacteria, researchers relied on sequencing the 16S rRNA gene of all bacterial DNA in each sample. Slight variations in the sequence of this gene revealed different species of bacteria. The researchers resampled the volunteers at three different times during the study to see if their microbiomes had changed. The investigators ended up with a deluge of data.

Before the NIH study, researchers had identified only a few hundred species of bacteria from the human body. This time, using the most advanced DNA-based methods, scientists identified about ten thousand species of microbes, including many that had never been seen before. Those ten thousand or so species had more than eight million genes among them. That's more than three hundred times the number of human genes—roughly twenty-five thousand—in a single human body.

The study revealed that each person carries a unique microbiome. No two people harbor the same set of microbes. Scientists think the differences are caused by variations in diet, environment, and the host's own genes. Yet even with differences among individual microbiomes, similar body parts have similar microbes. Armpit microbes from one person are similar to armpit microbes from another person, for instance. Gut microbes in one person are like those of another person, although the two sets are not necessarily identical.

The researchers also discovered that although the microbes in a certain body part might vary from person to person, the microbes there still perform the same jobs. Some of the bacteria in the human gut, for instance, digest fats. Different species of gut microbes might digest fats in different people, but each healthy person has the necessary microbes to carry out the job. "It appears that bacteria can pinch hit for each other," says Curtis Huttenhower of the Harvard School of Public Health in Massachusetts. "It matters whether the [ability to do the job] is present, not which microbial species provides it."

DOWN THE HATCH

The NIH study identified a variety of microbes in the human mouth and gut. From a person's two front teeth to the esophagus to the large intestine, the human digestive tract is lined with microbes. Roughly one hundred to two hundred species live in the mouth. Different communities of microbes live in different parts of the mouth—on the tongue, on the gums, and on each tooth. The place where each tooth meets the gum is teeming with microbes. Many of these bugs are anaerobic, meaning they thrive in conditions where oxygen is low or absent altogether. Oxygen may even kill some of these microbes. The microbes in the mouth help digest the food humans eat, but they can also cause gum disease, cavities, and bad breath.

The microbes that live in your gut are relatively diverse. The typical colon is home to at least 160 different species of microbes. These are fairly consistent from person to person. These bacteria make essential nutrients and vitamins, produce agents that regulate immunity (the ability of the body to resist disease), and help break down foods that people otherwise could not digest.

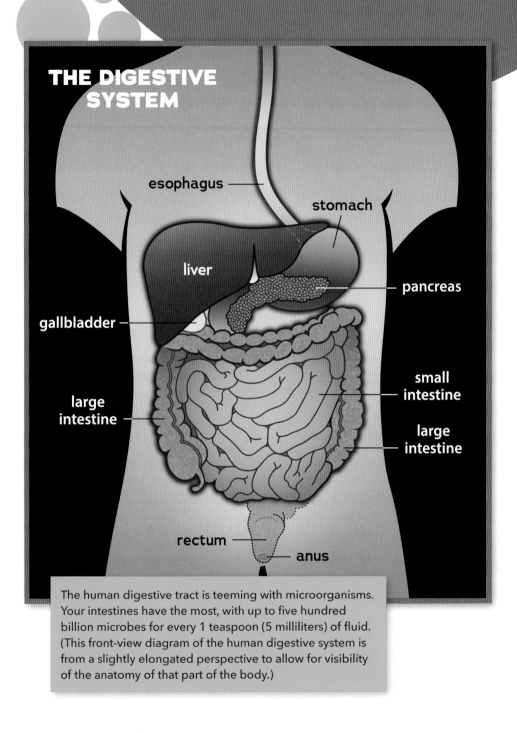

THE DIGESTIVE SYSTEM

esophagus

stomach

liver

pancreas

gallbladder

small intestine

large intestine

large intestine

rectum

anus

The human digestive tract is teeming with microorganisms. Your intestines have the most, with up to five hundred billion microbes for every 1 teaspoon (5 milliliters) of fluid. (This front-view diagram of the human digestive system is from a slightly elongated perspective to allow for visibility of the anatomy of that part of the body.)

Bacteria line the esophagus and thrive in the stomach, which is home to more than one hundred species of microbes. One of these species is *Helicobacter pylori*, which plays a role in producing acid to digest food and to kill most of the foreign bacteria that arrive on the food. Just past the stomach, huge numbers of microbes crawl in the small intestine. The microbes that live in your gut are relatively diverse. The typical colon is home to at least 160 different species of microbes. These are fairly consistent from person to person. These bacteria make essential nutrients and vitamins, produce agents that regulate immunity (the ability of the body to resist disease), and help break down foods that people otherwise could not digest.

Skin in the Game

The NIH study found that human skin teems with communities of microbes. You'll find microbes on the surface of your skin, in your pores and sweat glands, and along strands of your hair. Different patches of skin can have very different environments— dry, moist, or oily—and are therefore home to very different communities of microbes. Compare a sweaty armpit with a dry forearm with a greasy forehead. These three areas of skin are as different as a rain forest, a desert, and a swamp. These differences may be why certain skin diseases pop up at some places on the body and not others. For instance, *Propionibacterium acnes*, the bacteria species that has a role in the development of acne, thrives in oily areas such as the forehead but not in dry places such as the forearm.

Microbes on the skin help keep potential pathogens on the skin from growing out of control. They also produce a moisturizing layer that helps keep the skin soft and free from cracks, so that pathogens cannot enter the body through these slight openings. Microbes also live in openings in the skin—in the eyes, ears, nose,

PREDOMINANT BACTERIA IN ADULTS

Anatomical location	Predominant bacteria
Skin	*Staphylococci* and *Corynebacteria*
Eyes	Gram-positive cocci and gram-negative rods
Teeth	*Streptococci* and *Lactobacilli*
Mucous membranes in mouth	*Streptococci* and lactic acid bacteria
Nasal membranes	*Staphylococci* and *Corynebacteria*
Throat	*Streptococci*, *Neisseria*, gram-negative rods, and gram-negative cocci
Lower respiratory tract	none
Stomach	*Helicobacter pylori*
Small intestine	Lactic acid bacteria, enteric bacteria, *Enterococci*, and *Bifidobacteria*
Colon	*Bacteroides*, lactic acid bacteria, enteric bacteria, *Enterococci*, *Clostridia*, and methanogens
Urinary tract	*Staphylococci*, *Corynebacteria*, and enteric bacteria
Vagina (during childbearing years)	Lactic acid bacteria

mouth, and genital areas. These hidden residents are important to human health because they take up space that harmful microbes might otherwise fill.

A GIFT FROM MOM

Where does your microbiome come from? According to the NIH and other studies, childbirth may be the event that kicks it all off. In preparation for childbirth, a pregnant mother's body begins to change and the diversity of vaginal bacteria shifts. Abundant species become rare, and certain rare species flourish. One rare group that flourishes during pregnancy is the genus *Lactobacillus*. These bacteria can digest lactose, the major sugar in breast milk. Scientists suspect that the various changes in a pregnant woman's microbiome may allow the mother to transfer a special set of beneficial microbes to her baby.

During childbirth, babies move from the mother's womb through her birth canal. The birth canal is flexible, like a rubber glove. As the baby moves through it, the birth canal touches each part of the baby, coating the skin, nose, and mouth with vaginal microbes. This process exposes the baby to a rich mix of

THE NOT-SO-STERILE WOMB

For a long time, scientists and physicians thought the womb was sterile—completely free of microbes. But new studies contradict this idea and provide evidence that newborns encounter their first microbes before birth. In healthy pregnant women, microbes have been found in the placenta, the organ that feeds the growing fetus during pregnancy. They have also been found in the umbilical cord, which connects the baby to the placenta, and in the amniotic fluid, which surrounds the baby in the womb. Researchers have also found microbes in the first feces of babies born prematurely. Scientists believe that these microbes are acquired in the womb, because they appear before babies have eaten their first meals.

If the human microbiome does indeed begin to develop before birth, when and how do microbes begin to move from the mother to the baby? Are mothers delivering a random set of microbes or a special set that will benefit the developing fetus? What role do these microbes play in the health and development of the fetus? Scientists are still studying these questions to learn more about the development of the human microbiome.

maternal microbes, including milk-digesting *Lactobacillus*. "Being slathered in vaginal microbes might not seem like much of a treat," writes science journalist Ed Yong. "But to a newborn, it's a key event."

Immediately after childbirth, the baby instinctively reaches its mouth—now full of *Lactobacillus*—toward its mother's nipple and begins to suck. In addition to nutrients for the baby, breast milk is full of sugars called oligosaccharides. The milk is also full of specific microbes that eat these sugars, such as *Bifidobacterium infantis*. The purpose of the sugars is to support *B. infantis* and other important microbes as they move into and colonize the newborn's gut. In other words, the sugars feed the microbes, not the baby. These microbes are important for the baby's developing immune system. So when babies breastfeed, they not only receive nutrition, they also get a starter set of bacteria and the food needed to nourish them.

The First Year of Life

Studies have revealed that the microbiome changes over the first year of life. The early colonizing microbes—acquired during childbirth and breastfeeding—kick off a dynamic process as the microbiome grows and changes along with the growing, changing child.

As babies are held, kissed, and played with, they are introduced—through touch—to new, helpful microbes. Every kiss or hug from mother, father, siblings, and other caregivers contributes more microbes. As months go by, babies pick up more microbes from their environment. They crawl on the floor. They get a tongue lick from the family dog. They pick up a toy and put it in their mouths.

Babies also acquire microbes from their food. At each stage, the baby's microbial community reflects the food he or she is

MAPPING THE FIRST YEAR OF LIFE

To study how microbes in the human intestine change over the first year of life, researchers at Stanford University in California recruited parents to participate in a yearlong study of their babies. During diaper changes, parents collected samples of babies' feces and stored them in their home freezers until they could be moved to the lab. Parents also kept a journal, recording key events in their babies' lives, such as illness, medical treatments, diet changes, and travel. Investigators then analyzed DNA from each fecal sample. The researchers published their results in 2007. They were able to develop a picture of the types of gut microbes that were present throughout the first year of life. By the end of the first year, all of the babies' gut communities were well on their way to looking like that of an adult.

In another study, published in 2011, researchers followed one baby boy for more than two years, tracking changes in his health and diet and analyzing his feces to learn more about the development of his microbiome. The researchers observed that the number and variety of bacteria changed when the boy had a fever, ate new foods, or took antibiotics. They also observed that the bacteria changed with the introduction of solid foods. As the child aged, the microbial mix began to look more like that of an adult. The experiment showed that shifts in the microbiome were associated with specific life events.

eating. At first, the mix of microbes depends on whether the baby drinks breast milk or formula. Breast-fed babies end up with high amounts of *Bifidobacteria infantis*, the sugar-digesting bacteria in mother's milk. Formula-fed babies end up with less *Bifidobacteria*. One group of bacteria, the Bacteroidetes, flourishes when babies start to eat bananas, mashed peas, and other solid foods. This group specializes in breaking down complex carbohydrates from plant foods.

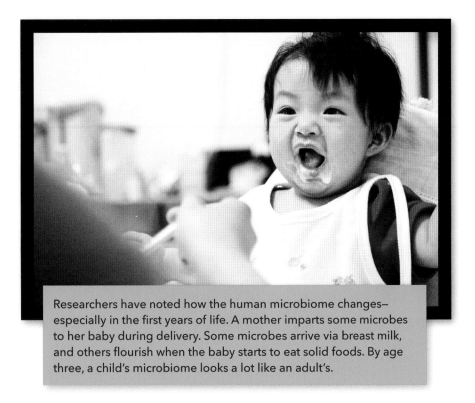

Researchers have noted how the human microbiome changes—especially in the first years of life. A mother imparts some microbes to her baby during delivery. Some microbes arrive via breast milk, and others flourish when the baby starts to eat solid foods. By age three, a child's microbiome looks a lot like an adult's.

Each baby's microbiome is personal and unique, like a fingerprint. Some of the variation between babies happens because infants pick up microbes from their families and surroundings, with the microbes of each family and environment being different. Scientists think that the baby's genes may be involved, helping some microbes to grow while discouraging others, although how and why this happens is not well understood.

As the child grows, the microbiome becomes more complex. By the age of three, the child's microbial community looks a lot like an adult's. At this age, differences between children shrink and their microbiomes become more similar.

7

Mixed-Up Microbes

A healthy immune system is like a team of Secret Service agents inside the White House. The team's job is to spot and fight off dangerous invaders without harming the president, the First Family, or their guests. In the same way, the body's immune system must be ready to deal with invaders, but it must not go overboard and harm the body's cells, tissues, organs, or beneficial microbes. Finding the right balance is critical. If the immune system is too gentle, it won't recognize and react to dangerous infections. If it is too robust, it may overreact to something harmless. Allergies and asthma are signs of an overactive immune system. So are autoimmune diseases such as multiple sclerosis, inflammatory bowel disease (IBD), and type 1 diabetes. In these diseases, the immune system attacks cells in the body by mistake.

You probably know people who have food allergies, hay fever, or asthma. You may even occasionally itch, sneeze, or wheeze yourself. In the United States, rates of asthma and allergies have tripled since the 1980s. These diseases happen when the immune system overreacts to something harmless.

Allergies and asthma were once rare. There's no mention of allergies in ancient historical records. As for asthma, the ancient Greeks knew of it only as a condition triggered by exercise, never dust or pollen. In seventeenth-century Europe, asthma and allergies were known but were rare.

By the beginning of the twentieth century, both conditions had become common in people living in Europe, North America, and other "WEIRD" areas. (Scientists use the acronym WEIRD in reference to people in *W*estern, *e*ducated, *i*ndustrialized, *r*ich, and *d*emocratic nations.) By the 1980s, asthma had become the most common chronic, or ongoing, disease in American children. In the twenty-first century, allergies and asthma plague 20 percent of Americans. One-quarter of those people suffer symptoms severe enough to trigger anaphylaxis. This reaction can include swelling and closing of the throat, lung spasms, and a drop in blood pressure. It can even lead to death.

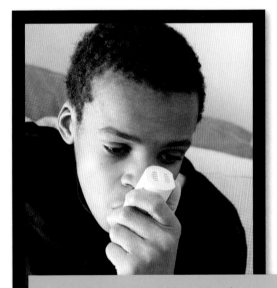

In the industrialized world, more and more young people must use inhalers to treat symptoms of asthma. Scientists think that the increase in asthma might be linked to microbes. They note that kids with asthma have different gut microbes than kids without asthma.

In WEIRD countries, starting in the early twentieth century, the human immune system appears to have grown more likely to overreact. A large body of research links the rising rates of allergies and asthma to less exposure to microbes.

THE HYGIENE HYPOTHESIS

On November 9, 1989, Germans tore down the Berlin Wall—a barrier that since 1961 had separated the city of Berlin into eastern and western sections. (Democratic West Germany ruled the western section, and Communist East Germany ruled the eastern section.) The following year, East Germany and West Germany reunited as one nation, and the unified city of Berlin became its new capital.

For Erika von Mutius, a West German physician treating patients with debilitating childhood asthma, the reunification of Germany presented an exciting opportunity. Von Mutius wanted to know why rates of asthma and allergies had risen dramatically in WEIRD nations. She thought the answer had something to do with lifestyle.

The reunification of Germany allowed von Mutius to study and compare children from East Germany and West Germany—two groups who were ethnically similar and thus had similar genes but who lived very different lifestyles. At the time, many East German cities were poor and polluted. West German cities tended to be wealthier, more modern, and cleaner. Von Mutius thought that children growing up in the dirtier cities of East Germany would suffer more wheezing and sneezing than youngsters in the cleaner cities of West Germany.

The exact opposite turned out to be true. Von Mutius's studies showed that children in dirty East Germany had lower rates of asthma and allergies than children in gleaming West Germany. Her research suggested that the explosion in asthma and allergies in West Germany was linked not to pollution but to children's lack of early exposure to microbes that strengthen the immune system. This idea has been dubbed the hygiene hypothesis. The hygiene hypothesis says that it's good to be exposed to microbes, especially early in life. It says that if you limit young children's exposure to microbes, they are less likely to build robust immune systems and are more likely to develop overactive systems that are susceptible to allergies or asthma.

KIDS AND CRITTERS

Scientists have found three factors linked to lower rates of allergic disease: big families, day care, and barnyard animals. Children who are around other children early in life—either because they grow up with older siblings or because they go to day care—are less likely to suffer from asthma and allergies. Scientists think these kids get exposed to microbes from other children, and this helps strengthen their immune systems. At the time of von Mutius's study, almost all East German mothers were working and their children were going to day care.

Exposure to animals helps too. A number of studies have shown that children in farm families have very low rates of allergy and asthma, while children in cities have much higher rates. Further study has revealed that the biggest benefit of farm living comes from animals. It appears that spending time around farm animals dramatically lowers risks of asthma and allergies. Researchers believe that children gain protection by being exposed to a wide range of microbes from livestock. And the more microbes the better. Investigators have tallied the number of microbes in dust from animal stables at different farms. Kids on the farms with the most microbes in the dust have the lowest rates of allergy and asthma.

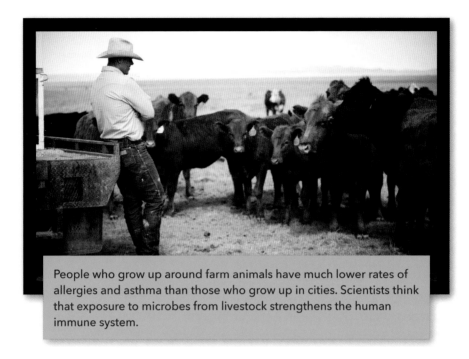

People who grow up around farm animals have much lower rates of allergies and asthma than those who grow up in cities. Scientists think that exposure to microbes from livestock strengthens the human immune system.

In addition, researchers have observed that kids with allergies have different gut microbes than kids without allergies, but whether the allergic kids' microbes lead to the allergies or the allergies change the microbes is still being investigated. In one study, researchers identified four genuses of gut microbes that were missing in young children who later went on to develop debilitating asthma. The four types of bacteria (*Lachnospira*, *Veillonella*, *Faecalibacterium*, and *Rothia*) were abundant in the guts of healthy children. In the same study, when researchers gave the four kinds of bacteria to mice with an asthma-like condition, the animals' asthma symptoms went away. That's evidence that the microbes protect against asthma.

MISTAKEN IDENTITY

In allergies and asthma, the immune system overreacts to something harmless. These aren't the only immune disorders skyrocketing in the twenty-first century. Autoimmune diseases have also risen dramatically. In autoimmune diseases, the immune system becomes confused and attacks the body's own tissues as if they were harmful invaders. It is a classic case of mistaken identity. Scientists think that disruptions in the gut microbiome may be involved in autoimmune disorders such as type 1 diabetes and IBD.

In type 1 diabetes, the immune system destroys insulin-producing cells in the pancreas. As a result, type 1 diabetics lack insulin, a hormone that allows glucose (sugar) in the blood to enter cells in the body, where it is metabolized for energy. Without insulin, tissues and cells in the body starve, even though the blood is full of sugar. Over time, high levels of sugar in the blood can damage a range of body tissues, such as the heart, nerves, skin, and kidneys. If untreated, the disease can be fatal. (Type 1 diabetes is different from type 2 diabetes, in which the body produces insulin but is unable to use it properly. Type 2 diabetes usually develops in adults, while type 1 diabetes develops more commonly in young people.)

The rate of type 1 diabetes in the WEIRD world is rising, and the disease is appearing in younger and younger children. Although type 1 diabetes is strongly influenced by genes, rates are rising faster than can be explained by genetics alone. Scientists believe that something in the environment is triggering the development of type 1 diabetes in more children and at younger ages. That trigger might be a change in the microbiome. In one study, researchers noted that before people developed type 1 diabetes, their gut microbiomes became less diverse. Other studies have shown that the gut microbiome of a healthy person is different from that of someone with type 1 diabetes.

Like type 1 diabetes, IBD (a condition that includes Crohn's disease and ulcerative colitis) is also growing more common.

THE STRANGE CASE OF THE DISAPPEARING *HELICOBACTER PYLORI*

Helicobacter pylori are curved-shaped bacteria that have lived in the spongy lining of the human stomach for thousands of years. In fact, they are the most common type of bacteria in the stomach. However, *H. pylori* is disappearing in the stomachs of people in the United States. Physician Martin Blaser of New York University's Langone Medical Center has led an investigation into the disappearance. "Most people born in the United States in the early twentieth century carried the organism. But fewer than six percent of children born after 1995 have it in their stomachs," he notes.

Scientists know that *H. pylori* can make people sick. In some people, it can cause gastric cancer and gastric ulcers, painful sores on the inside of the stomach or small intestine. The discovery of the link between *H. pylori* and disease earned a Nobel Prize for two Australian researchers in 2005. Because of the association with cancer and ulcers, it may seem like a good thing that this kind of bacteria is disappearing. But most people with *H. pylori* do not develop gastric ulcers or gastric cancer, and in fact, *H. pylori* can also keep people healthy. It has a role in helping children develop a healthy immune system. Studies have shown that children with *H. pylori* are less likely to develop asthma and certain allergies than those without *H. pylori*.

Why is *H. pylori* disappearing? One reason is better sanitation. In places without clean running water, indoor plumbing, and sewage treatment plants, *H. pylori* can pass from person to person through drinking water that has been contaminated with human feces. Improved sanitation cuts down on this transmission. Although clean water is undoubtedly a good thing and has enormous benefits for public health, it can have the hidden consequence of altering our microbiomes. Some scientists think antibiotic overuse could also be contributing to *H. pylori's* gradual disappearance.

In patients with an IBD, chronic inflammation can damage the intestine and cause vomiting, diarrhea, and anemia (low iron). In severe cases, surgeons must remove damaged parts of the intestine. Genes and diet play a role in IBD, but scientists believe that something beyond genetics is contributing to the rising rates of this family of diseases.

As with type 1 diabetes, the gut microbiome of a healthy person is different from that of someone with IBD. For instance, a person with IBD has less microbial diversity as well as fewer types of Firmicutes and Bacteroidetes—two major groups of gut bacteria that are essential for digesting different kinds of foods. (Firmicutes digest a range of nutrients and may promote absorption of fat by the body. Bacteroidetes are good at digesting complex carbohydrates from plants.)

Although gut microbes seem to be linked to some autoimmune diseases, that association does not necessarily mean that the gut microbes cause the diseases. While some researchers think gut microbes could be the cause, others wonder if the gut's microbial community shifts after the onset of the disease. Or something else entirely could be causing both the change in microbes and the diseases themselves. Researchers are trying to pin down if and how specific microbes might influence the development of diabetes, IBD, and other autoimmune diseases. If scientists are able to prove that a change in the microbiome precedes the onset of such a disease, future research will likely focus on finding treatments to shift microbial communities to a healthier state.

OBESE MICE, THIN MICE

As with rising rates of autoimmune diseases, obesity rates have soared in the United States. Obesity is a condition in which a person's body weight is at least 20 percent higher than what is considered healthy for that person's age and height. In 1980, 14 percent of US adults were obese. By 2013 the number had more than doubled, with more than 34 percent of adults classified as obese. The problem is not just with adults. Among US children and adolescents, 17 percent are obese.

While eating too much and exercising too little contribute to obesity, the causes of obesity are far more complex. Genes contribute to obesity, as does a person's home environment. For instance, children in poor households are more likely to be obese than children in wealthy families. One reason is because food options tend to be limited in poor neighborhoods, with more convenience stores and fast-food chains selling inexpensive, high-calorie foods and with fewer full-service grocery stores and farmers' markets selling healthy foods. Also wielding influence over obesity are the microbes that live in the human gut. Studies show that obese people have different microbial communities in their guts than thin people. For example, obese people have fewer Bacteroidetes and more Firmicutes. Recall that Bacteroidetes in the gut digest complex plant carbohydrates, while Firmicutes may promote absorption of fat, which might explain why those with more Firmicutes gain weight. Obese people also have less diverse microbial gut communities overall than thin people. Researchers have observed that when obese individuals lose weight, the makeup of their gut microbiome shifts and resembles that of a thin person's microbiome.

Studies like these show a clear link between the microbiome and obesity, but they don't reveal cause and effect. Do differences in the microbiome contribute to obesity? Or do different microbes settle in after a person is already obese? The answer is important. If the microbiome changes first, scientists might eventually find ways to influence the microbiome to help people better control their weight.

To probe cause and effect, researchers have turned to mice. Like humans, obese mice and thin mice have different microbial communities in their guts. Scientists have studied these differences using germ-free mice (mice without microbes of their own) and fecal transplants. For the transplants, researchers took feces from mice with microbes and transplanted it into the guts of germ-free mice. Revolting? Perhaps. But also revealing.

When scientists gave germ-free mice fecal transplants, using "thin microbes" from thin mice or "obese microbes" from obese mice, the mice that received obese microbes gained more weight than those that received thin microbes. Both sets of mice ate the same amount of food, so the difference was not caused by food intake. Instead, it appears that the obese microbes extracted more energy from the food and signaled the body to store the extra energy as fat. In a different experiment, germ-free mice that received obese microbes exhibited changed behavior: they ate more and gained more weight.

To learn about obesity in humans, scientists study the microbiomes of obese mice. The Jackson Laboratory, with branches in Maine, Connecticut, and California, breeds mice with specific traits—such as obesity—and ships them to researchers around the world for further study.

Obesity and thinness can even be passed from people to mice. In another study, scientists took fecal samples from human twins—one of them obese and the other a healthy weight—and transplanted them into germ-free mice. Mice that received microbes from the obese twin gained more weight and put on more fat than those that received thin microbes. If researchers can identify specific microbes that transfer thinness, they might be able to create a probiotic—a blend of beneficial bacteria—that together with a defined diet could prevent weight gain.

THE ROLE OF ANTIBIOTICS

Scientists believe that allergies, asthma, autoimmune diseases, and obesity are all associated with changes or differences in the makeup of human microbes. Could antibiotics—which are routinely used to change the human microbiome to prevent and treat infection—also be fueling epidemics of these diseases? Researchers are actively investigating this question, and in some cases, the answer appears to be yes. For example, a number of studies have linked childhood asthma to use of antibiotics. One study followed more than thirteen thousand children over a number of years and found that children were more likely to develop asthma if they had taken antibiotics in the first seven years of life. The risk was highest in children who had received four or more courses of antibiotics. This study does not establish that antibiotics caused asthma, and indeed other studies have questioned the link. In addition to human studies, studies in mice show that mice that receive certain antibiotics early in life develop more food allergies than untreated mice.

What about obesity? In a sense, the connection between antibiotics and obesity has already been made—in farm animals. For decades farmers in the United States have fed low doses of antibiotics to their animals to promote weight gain. Scientists don't know why or how this works, but the earlier in life the animals begin to receive antibiotics, the more weight they gain. Scientists have also tested this connection in mice, finding that antibiotics early in life contribute to obesity. Young mice that receive antibiotics become fatter than mice that do not. Follow-up experiments in mice with fecal transplants have been revealing as well. Using fecal transplants, researchers placed either antibiotic-treated microbes or untreated microbes into the guts of germ-free mice. The mice that received antibiotic-treated microbes became heavier and fatter.

But do antibiotics have the same effect in people? Scientists do not yet know, but experiments to determine whether there is a link between antibiotic use and obesity in people are under way.

COLONIZATION GONE WRONG

Scientists do know that babies born by cesarean sections, or C-sections (surgical births), are more likely to suffer from health problems than are babies born vaginally, or through the birth canal. C-sections are often medically necessary. In some instances, a C-section may save the life of the mother or her child. But rates of C-sections have risen dramatically in the twenty-first century. For example, some women and doctors choose C-sections because a woman fears the pain of childbirth or wants to schedule the birth at a convenient time. In the United States, nearly one-third of babies are delivered by C-section.

Scientists know that passage through the birth canal is a key event in the healthy development of a baby's microbiome.

OVERSELLING THE MICROBIOME

"Changes in the Gut Bacteria Protect against Stroke." "The Microbiome: Your Key to Glowing Skin & Healthy Weight." "Fast-Metabolism Microbes: The 20-Day Plan That Will Change the Way You Burn Fat Forever." Don't believe headlines such as these. On the Internet and in other media sources, you are likely to see plenty of hype about the microbiome. In 2010 Jonathan Eisen, a microbiologist at the University of California–Davis, created the Overselling the Microbiome Award. He regularly gives it to people and organizations that, in his opinion, exaggerate the results of research studies or make misleading claims about the microbiome. "We have gone from everyone ignoring the 'cloud' of microbes that live in and on various plants and animals," writes Eisen, "to everyone now basically implying that the microbiomes do EVERYTHING."

Human health is complicated, and the microbiome is not the only factor in controlling health and disease. Eisen stresses that correlation does not equal causation. That is, just because two things occur together does not mean one thing causes the other. In fact, one of the major challenges in microbiome research is determining when a microbe is actually causing a disease or symptom and when it is just a bystander.

Babies that travel through the birth canal are colonized mainly with bacteria from the mother's vagina. These bacteria include those of the genus *Lactobacillus*, which help babies digest milk and which become early colonizers of the gut. What happens if a baby doesn't pass through the vagina at birth? Studies show that C-section babies are colonized instead by bacteria more commonly found on skin, such as *Staphylococcus* bacteria. Some of these bacteria come from the mother's skin, but others seem to be picked up from the doctors and nurses who deliver the baby and from the hospital surroundings.

Antibiotic-resistant strains of *Staphylococcus*, such as MRSA, can cause infection in babies in hospital delivery wards. In one California study carried out in 2004, between 64 and 82 percent of newborns with MRSA infections had been delivered by C-section. Scientists think that bacteria passed down from mother to child during a vaginal delivery may form a protective shield on the child's skin, helping ward off MRSA and other dangerous microbes. Babies born by C-section lack that shield, making them more vulnerable to infection.

Studies have also shown that babies born by C-section are more likely to suffer from obesity, asthma, allergies, and autoimmune problems as they grow to adulthood. One prominent explanation is that babies who have not been colonized by the optimal set of maternal microbes at birth are more likely to have compromised immune systems. Researchers are investigating this idea by swabbing some children delivered by C-sections with vaginal fluid from their mothers immediately after birth and then monitoring the children's health over the long term. Time will tell whether steps like these can replace microbes that would otherwise be missing and deliver long-term benefits to a child's health.

8

PROTECTING THE MICROBIOME

Since the first decade of the twenty-first century, the trillions of microbes that live in the human body have become one of the hottest areas of medical research. Not long ago, many fundamental questions about the microbiome were difficult or impossible to answer. With metagenomics—the study of all the genetic material in a specific sample—our understanding is moving ahead by leaps and bounds. Scientists can find answers to questions such as, How many microbes dwell at a given body site? How does the microbiome vary from person to person? Is there a core set of microbes that we all share?

As answers pour in, scientists are beginning to move to even deeper questions: How do our genes influence our microbes? How does our microbiome change as we gain or lose weight, take a course of antibiotics, get sick, or grow old?

Researchers can compare microbes in different people—sick people versus healthy people, people who took antibiotics as children versus people who didn't—to see if there are differences in the microbiomes of each group. Ultimately, scientists will be able to understand exactly how a specific microbe or mix of microbes contributes to health. The long-term goal is to use that information to encourage or discourage the growth of certain microbes to improve human health. But this will not be easy. "Fixing a microbiome is not like popping a pill to treat a vitamin deficiency. It is a feat of ecological engineering, an attempt to repair a damaged ecosystem," says science journalist Ed Yong. "You cannot do that without knowing what the default 'healthy' state looks like: which species were lost, what roles they played, how they interact with one another, or how to bring them back."

Scientists can't yet say with any confidence what a healthy microbiome looks like. In many cases, it's not the specific microbes that are present in any particular body but the overall diversity of the microbial ecosystem that seems to lead to good health. In all likelihood, a one-size-fits-all healthy microbiome does not exist.

A LITTLE LESS WEIRD

One way to improve our understanding of the microbiome is to expand the reach of microbiome studies and to gain a better picture of microbial diversity. So far, most microbial studies have focused on Europe, North America, and other WEIRD parts of the world. That means that most of the microbes that scientists are studying come from people who live in wealthy, industrialized countries.

WEIRD people represent just 12 percent of the world's population, so their microbes don't reflect the global human microbiome.

SOLVING MURDERS WITH MICROBES

You have probably heard of using DNA to solve crimes. Investigators can collect DNA from a strand of hair or drop of blood at a crime scene to identify a victim or a suspect. Could microbes be used in a similar way?

Each person has a unique microbial community—a microbial fingerprint. Researchers can identify people based on their microbes, and they can link those microbes to objects people have touched. For instance, researchers can identify someone who used a computer keyboard by sampling the millions of microbes on a single key and then comparing them to a selection of microbial samples from other people to look for a match. Someday researchers envision being able to compare microbes using a huge database of samples from many people. This technique, which has not yet been developed, could be used to link a suspect to a murder weapon or to place someone at the scene of a crime.

Microbes could help in murder investigations in other ways. Microbes play an important role in the decomposition of dead bodies. As a body decomposes, bacteria and fungi change in predictable ways over time. If researchers can better understand these changes and how long they take, they can help answer an important question in a murder investigation: When did the victim die?

Researchers already use other methods to pinpoint time of death. For example, investigators know how long it takes certain species of flies to complete their life cycle—from egg to larva to pupa to winged adult—and this information can help establish how long a corpse has been exposed to insects, thus establishing time since death. Using bacteria in a similar way would give researchers an additional tool to establish time of death, particularly in cases where insects are not present.

Investigators have achieved this analysis with mice. They have found that changes in microbes on a mouse corpse are measurable and predictable. They have been able to trace when a mouse died to within a three-day window over a forty-eight-day period.

Many aspects of modern life in WEIRD nations—antibiotic use, C-sections, and high-calorie diets—shift microbial communities in ways that are linked to obesity, allergies, and diabetes. What do microbial communities look like in people who do not live a WEIRD lifestyle?

To find out, researchers visited villages in rural Africa and ventured deep into the Amazon rain forest of South America. They swabbed skin and collected fecal samples from rural villagers and hunter-gatherers—people who get their food by killing wild animals and gathering wild plants. The hunter-gatherers under study included the Yanomami of Venezuela, the Matsés of Peru, and the Hadza of Tanzania. The researchers compared the samples from villagers and hunter-gatherers with samples from European and American city dwellers.

The research revealed that the microbiomes of people in the West (the industrialized world) look very different from those of rural peoples in Africa and South America. The microbes of non-Western people are significantly more diverse. For instance, Amazon hunter-gatherers harbor twice as many microbial species in their guts and on their skin as do US city dwellers.

Why the differences in microbial diversity? Rural villagers and hunter-gatherers live in a less urbanized environment and have more exposure to microbes from animals, plants, and soil. They tend to have large families, which give children plenty of interaction with siblings, cousins, grandparents, aunts, and uncles and expose them to a greater variety of microbes. They also don't encounter the microbe-killing antibiotics of the West.

In numerous research studies and across many different health problems, greater microbial diversity has consistently been associated with better health. Does that mean that the rural Africans and South Americans are healthier than Westerners? No, but they do have lower rates of the health problems

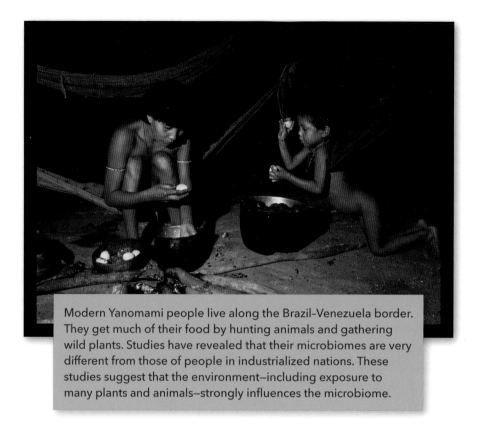

Modern Yanomami people live along the Brazil–Venezuela border. They get much of their food by hunting animals and gathering wild plants. Studies have revealed that their microbiomes are very different from those of people in industrialized nations. These studies suggest that the environment–including exposure to many plants and animals–strongly influences the microbiome.

associated with a modern lifestyle, such as autoimmune diseases and allergies.

People in the West also eat differently than non-Westerners, and these differences show up in their guts. The bacterial communities of Europeans and North Americans are full of species that are good at digesting simple sugars (found in processed food) and amino acids (found in high-protein dairy products and meat). But the guts of non-Westerners—who eat more plants and very little meat—are loaded with bacterial species that can digest tough plant carbohydrates. This suggests that what we eat has a big influence on our microbiomes.

At one time, hundreds of years ago, people in the Western world had larger families and lived in rural areas, more like the modern-day villagers and hunter-gatherers who were studied in Africa and South America. At that time, the Western and non-Western microbiomes were probably similar. But the twenty-first-century Western lifestyle has yielded a changed microbiome, one dominated by fewer bacterial species overall and by less diversity. Some scientists believe that humans might be healthier if the lost bacterial species and greater diversity were restored.

ANTIBIOTICS: WEIGHING RISKS AND BENEFITS

The benefit of antibiotics is clear: they stop serious bacterial infections, and they prevent infections during surgery and in the treatment of diseases like cancer. They have saved millions of lives since they were first introduced in the mid-twentieth century. Yet these lifesaving drugs can also do harm. Antibiotics can kill helpful microbes in the human body, and antibiotics are contributing—through overuse—to the evolution of dangerous, antibiotic-resistant bacteria. Antibiotics change the environment in which bacteria grow and create conditions in which resistant bacteria survive, reproduce, and become more common.

Many doctors and patients in the United States and elsewhere treat antibiotics as wonder drugs with few risks. Patients frequently request—and doctors routinely prescribe—antibiotics for minor infections that are likely to clear up on their own as well as for viral illnesses on which antibiotics have no effect. Martin Blaser of New York University explains the rationale for the casual approach to antibiotics: "'Why don't we just give some antibiotics, because it can't hurt?' That's how people think—doctors and patients alike." But in fact, it can hurt.

"The use of antibiotics is the single most important factor leading to antibiotic resistance around the world," according to a report on US antibiotic use from the CDC. "Up to 50% of antibiotics prescribed for people are not needed or are not optimally effective as prescribed."

How can we receive the benefits of antibiotics while minimizing the risks? One step is to use antibiotics only when they are medically appropriate and to take them exactly as prescribed. Another is to limit the use of antibiotics in farm animals, which could help slow the evolution of dangerous drug-resistant bacteria in animals and the transmission of these bacteria to people. In countries that have restricted antibiotic use on farms, the level of resistant bacteria in humans appears to decrease over time.

Experts also recommend restricting the use of antibacterial products. In 2015 antibacterial chemicals could be found in soaps, hand sanitizers, toothpaste, cosmetics, household cleaners, cutting boards, sponges, countertops, and refrigerators. These products contain antibiotics, although they may be labeled instead with a term such as *antibacterial*. The products can kill broad swaths of dangerous microbes, but they can also kill beneficial microbes. And they encourage the evolution of antibiotic-resistant bacteria because antibacterial chemicals work similarly to medical antibiotics: too many leads to resistance.

Triclosan is one such antibacterial chemical. Manufacturers commonly add it to soaps, toothpastes, and cosmetics, as well as to clothing, furniture, and toys. This may improve sales among a germ-fearing public that looks for products to protect against illness. But triclosan's use over time has led to cross-resistance— that is, bacteria that evolve resistance to triclosan also are able to resist certain medical antibiotics.

According to the FDA, antibacterial soaps are not any more effective at preventing illness than are plain soaps. Starting in 2016, companies selling antibacterial products in the United States must prove to the FDA that these products are safe and are more effective at preventing illness and infection than soap and water.

MICROBES AND MALNUTRITION

Gut microbes contribute to malnutrition, a condition in which a person does not have enough of the necessary nutrients for life. Malnutrition involves more than just a lack of food. In kwashiorkor, a type of malnutrition common in Africa, malnourished children eat just as much as healthy children, but their bodies can't absorb the nutrients. The disease develops in young children who do not get enough protein as babies.

Scientists know that identical twins share the same genes. They usually share the same diet too. In some families, however, one twin may have kwashiorkor while the other twin is healthy. They differ only in their gut microbes. By combining studies of malnutrition in mice and human twins, researchers have identified a set of eleven microbes that together with poor diet damage the gut and contribute to kwashiorkor.

Someday doctors may develop ways of analyzing children's microbial communities before symptoms develop to know who is at risk of malnutrition. They may also be able to manipulate the microbiome to help at-risk children take in more nutrients from their food, so they can get the full value of everything they eat and lead healthier lives.

Children who suffer from kwashiorkor, such as this boy in the African nation of Malawi, cannot absorb all the nutrients in their food. The disease develops when young children don't get enough protein. It also involves specific microbes that damage the gut.

If manufacturers can't provide this proof, the FDA will require manufacturers to reformulate the products or pull them from store shelves.

THE PROMISE OF PROBIOTICS

Visit any grocery store, pharmacy, or health food store, and you'll find shelves crowded with probiotic foods and supplements. Probiotics are living microbes—such as *Lactobacillus*—that are similar to the beneficial microbes found naturally in the human body. They are commonly sold in pill form or are an added ingredient in foods such as yogurt. Doctors often recommend them as a way to add beneficial microbes to a person's microbiome. Related products known as prebiotics are foods or supplements that promote the growth of beneficial microbes. Probiotics are actual microbes, whereas prebiotics are foods or other products that nourish microbes. Prebiotics include asparagus, garlic, onions, Jerusalem artichokes, and dandelion root. Doctors are suggesting—and more and more people are buying and using—probiotics and prebiotics. In 2012 probiotics were a $26 billion industry worldwide. By 2019 the industry is expected to grow to $1.7 trillion.

But are prebiotics and probiotics worth taking? First, a dose of reality. Despite the hype about probiotics, it isn't scientifically clear what these products do for us or how much they can actually impact our microbiome. The FDA has not approved any health claims for probiotics. What's more, in the United States, most probiotics do not undergo the testing and approval process that medical drugs do, because probiotics are viewed as supplements, not medicine. Without government-backed testing, it's hard for consumers to know what they are really ingesting when they take probiotics. "It's the Wild West; the field is almost completely unregulated," writes Martin Blaser.

Probiotics appear to be safe for healthy people, but to be truly safe, check with your doctor before taking a probiotic. Probiotics can also help treat some health problems. For instance, they can relieve some types of diarrhea as well as some symptoms of irritable bowel syndrome, a common, chronic disorder of the large intestine. Researchers believe that probiotics also may reduce the risk of necrotizing enterocolitis, a life-threatening inflammation of the gut in premature infants. In the future, as researchers identify specific microbes that help specific conditions, doctors may be able to use probiotics to treat a wider variety of health problems, including obesity, malnutrition, and autoimmune disorders.

THE POWER OF POOP

Medical researchers have turned to human feces as one way to positively manipulate the human microbiome. For example, doctors are using fecal transplants to treat debilitating diarrhea. The procedure involves taking feces from a healthy human donor, straining it to remove solid matter and diluting it with liquid to create a solution filled with bacteria. The fecal solution is then transferred through a tube, via the rectum or the esophagus, into the gut of a person who is critically ill with diarrhea. This treatment has been remarkably effective at treating *C. diff,* the nasty, difficult-to-treat infection of the gut that causes severe diarrhea and kills thousands of people each year.

The standard treatment for *C. diff* is to give people a course of antibiotics to wipe out the infection, although this treatment does not always work. *C. diff* happens when strong antibiotics wipe out the normal gut microbiome. Treatment of a *C. diff* infection with more antibiotics likely fails because it doesn't restore a healthy gut ecosystem. Depending on the antibiotic used to treat *C. diff,* up to 35 percent of *C. diff* patients have a recurrence of the infection. A fecal transplant, on the other hand, can deliver a cure, sometimes in a single day. The donor bacteria fight off the *C. diff* bacteria, which have overrun the gut, and reestablish a normal, healthy, and balanced microbial community. Fecal transplants bring a complete recovery in 92 percent of people with recurring *C. diff* infections, a phenomenal success rate.

Although fecal transplants have not yet become mainstream medicine, they are being evaluated as a possible standard treatment for IBD and obesity. To ensure that patients will have access to fecal material for medical use, "poop banks"—similar to blood banks—have opened in cities around the world. There, healthy people can donate feces to be used in the future for treating sick people.

Researchers at Massachusetts General Hospital in Boston have even developed a "poop pill" to make treatment of *C. diff* easier than undergoing a fecal transplant. The pills are frozen, have no offensive odor, and are easy to swallow. Researchers began testing the pills on human volunteers in 2014 and are making the pills available to qualified patients with recurrent *C. diff* infections. Another research team, at the University of Western Ontario in Canada, is testing an experimental probiotic called RePOOPulate. This blend of thirty-three gut bacteria mimics the microbial community in a healthy gut and removes the feces from the treatment.

THE BACTERIA–BRAIN CONNECTION

As researchers continue to probe the role of the gut microbiome in health, they are finding unexpected connections. One link is the effect that gut microbes have on our brains.

Scientists have long known that the gut and brain talk to each other. If you've ever had a "gut feeling" about something or experienced "butterflies in your stomach" because you were

TENDING YOUR MICROBIAL GARDEN

You can take a few important steps to protect your microbial community.

- Take antibiotics only when medically appropriate. Don't ask your doctor for antibiotics when they are not needed. Complete a full course of antibiotics exactly as prescribed by your doctor. This will help curb the evolution of antibiotic-resistant bacteria in your body.

- Wash your hands regularly. Avoid soaps, lotions, and cleansers labeled "antibacterial" or "antimicrobial." If you can't wash with soap and water, use a nonantibiotic hand sanitizer, one that contains at least 60 percent alcohol. Alcohol-based hand sanitizers do not increase the chance of producing resistant bacteria.

- Eat a diverse diet high in fiber. Scientists believe that a diet rich in whole grains, fruits, and vegetables may support a healthy microbial community. Probiotics or fermented foods, both of which are high in microbes, may also help. Limit processed food, as some chemical additives have been shown to disturb our microbes. Finally, choose animal foods grown without antibiotics.

frightened or excited, you've felt this connection. The human gut contains more than one hundred million neurons, a vast web of nerves embedded in the lining of the esophagus, stomach, and small and large intestines. These nerves send signals directly through the vagus nerve, which connects the digestive tract and other internal organs to the central nervous system and the brain. Scientists call this "brain in the gut" the enteric nervous system. The conversation between gut and brain helps regulate appetite and affects mood.

Evidence is emerging that gut microbes are part of the conversation. Experiments show that germ-free mice, without any microbiome, behave differently than mice with intact microbiomes. The germ-free mice are more active, less anxious, and more likely to take risks. If germ-free baby mice are transplanted with intact mice microbiomes, they grow up to behave like normal mice: less active, more fearful. Changing the microbiome changes the behavior. But the transplant works only on baby mice. Adult mice that receive a transplant do not change their behavior, leading scientists to think that early microbial colonization shapes the way mice—and possibly people—think and behave.

Other research has linked the microbiome to autism, a neurodevelopmental disorder. People with autism range in the severity of their symptoms, but all have some degree of difficulty with social interaction and understanding nonverbal cues. Researchers are finding that the gut microbial communities of autistic children are different from those of non-autistic children. To learn more, scientists at the California Institute of Technology in Pasadena and the Baylor College of Medicine in Houston, Texas, studied mice with a disorder resembling autism. In results published in 2013, the scientists found that like autistic children, the "autistic" mice housed an altered microbial community in their guts compared to non-autistic mice. Autistic mice had lower levels of the beneficial microbe *Bacteroides fragilis* than did non-autistic mice. If investigators gave the mice *Bacteroides fragilis*, they displayed fewer autism-like behaviors. Again, changing the microbiome changed behavior.

How do gut microbes talk to the brain? Scientists aren't entirely sure. They could be sending signals through the vagus nerve. Or gut microbes—or perhaps the gut itself, in response to microbes—could be sending signaling molecules to the brain.

Immune cells could even be doing some of the talking. There is some evidence that they shuttle back and forth through the circulatory system between the gut and the brain.

The bacteria–brain research is still very new. We have a lot to learn. Already researchers have come a long way—from regarding all microbes as germs to be killed before they can spread to thinking of microbes as a possible miracle cure. The truth lies somewhere in between. Infectious pathogens do kill. But microbes can also benefit and heal us, in ways we are only beginning to discover. Many surprises await. In the meantime, we would be wise to take care of our invisible allies.

GLOSSARY

antibiotic: a drug that kills or slows the growth of microbes

antibiotic resistance: the natural ability of a microbe to resist one or more antibiotics. The ability may be acquired by mutation or by genes acquired from other microbes.

archaeon: a single-celled organism with no inner compartments. Scientists originally classified archaea as bacteria but then discovered that they have a different genetic and chemical makeup.

autism: a mental condition, present from early childhood, characterized by repetitive behaviors and difficulty in communication and social interaction. Scientists think that the gut microbes of autistic people might be different from those of non-autistic people and that changing these microbes might help treat autism.

bacterium: a single-celled organism with no inner compartments. Thousands of bacteria are part of the microbiome of humans and other animals.

Bacteroidetes: a group of bacteria that includes many species found in the human gut. Scientists believe they aid in digestion of complex carbohydrates from plants.

Bifidobacterium infantis: beneficial bacteria that live in the human gut, mouth, and vagina

Candida: a genus of yeasts that can cause fungal infections. Many species are commensals, microbes that benefit from living in our bodies but do not help or harm us.

chromosome: a structure in cells that is made of a large DNA molecule. The DNA of the chromosome contains genes, which hold instructions for how the organism will live and reproduce.

clinical trials: a scientific or medical experiment using human participants

Clostridium difficile: bacterium that live in the gut and can cause infectious diarrhea

coevolution: evolution involving two or more species, with the changes of one species bringing about changes in the other over roughly the same time frame

collapse: permanent and lasting damage to an ecosystem brought about by loss of diversity or by the loss of one key species

commensals: microbes that benefit from living inside our bodies but do not help or harm us

control group: a group in an experiment or study that does not receive treatment and then is compared to test subjects that do receive treatment. Researchers compare test subjects to control groups to measure the effectiveness of treatments.

deoxyribonucleic acid (DNA): the hereditary material that influences the development and characteristics of living things

diversity: the number of different species in an environment. Lack of diversity of the body's microbes has been associated with increased risk of health problems.

DNA sequencing: the process of determining the precise order of chemical units called nucleotides within a DNA molecule. Scientists do this by using technology to determine the order of the four bases—adenine, cytosine, guanine, and thymine—in a strand of DNA.

ecosystem: a biological community of living things and the environment in which they exist. The human body ecosystem includes the microbes and other tiny living things that live alongside and interact with human cells.

Enterococcus faecalis: bacteria that live in the human gut and that can cause potentially life-threating infection inside the body. _Enterococcus faecalis_ was responsible for transferring resistance to the antibiotic vancomycin to methicillin-resistant _Staphylococcus aureus_ (MRSA).

enzymes: proteins that bring about chemical reactions in organisms

Escherichia coli: a species of bacteria that lives in the human gut. At low levels, _Escherichia coli_ in the gut keep out harmful bacteria. But at high levels or found elsewhere inside the body, it can cause diarrhea or a deadly infection.

eukaryote: a living thing, such as a plant, animal, or fungus, whose cells contain a nucleus

evolution: the process by which organisms change over time, either randomly or in ways that enhance an organism's chance of reproduction and survival. These changes lead to the development of different species. The theory of evolution was first put forth by Charles Darwin, an English naturalist, in his book _On the Origin of the Species by Natural Selection_ (1859).

fermentation: a process by which microbes break down organic substances, changing their chemical makeup. Humans use fermentation to change the makeup of certain foods. For instance, grains can be fermented to make liquor, grapes can be fermented to make wine, and milk can be fermented to make cheese.

Firmicutes: a group of bacteria that includes the genuses _Staphylococcus_, _Streptococcus_, and _Lactobacillus_. Although many Firmicutes are a part of a healthy microbiome, some, such as *Clostridium difficile*, the bacteria that cause chronic, life-threatening diarrhea, can be harmful.

fungi: organisms that obtain food by absorbing it from other living things or from parts of formerly living things. Microscopic fungi are a part of the microbial community in your gut and on your skin. A few fungi can cause diseases.

gene: a segment of DNA that contains information regulating how an organism will live and reproduce

genetic code: the arrangement of chemicals in DNA that directs how an organism will grow and reproduce

germ: a microorganism that may or may not cause disease

germ-free animal: an animal that has no microorganisms living in or on it. Germ-free animals are created in a laboratory setting for the study of the microbiome.

germ theory of disease: the idea that some diseases are caused by microorganisms

***Helicobacter pylori*:** a species of bacteria that lives in the stomach and that can cause ulcers and other diseases in some people

horizontal gene transfer: a process by which bacteria pass plasmids back and forth to one another, thereby sharing DNA. Horizontal gene transfer allows bacteria to share antibiotic-resistant genes.

host: a living organism that provides a home for another organism. The host might provide the organism it houses with food or other benefits.

human microbiome: the collection of microbes on and inside the human body

hygiene hypothesis: the idea that it's good to be exposed to microbes, especially early in life, for the development of a robust immune system

immune system: a system of biological structures and processes in the body that protects against disease

inflammatory bowel diseases (IBD): a group of conditions involving inflammation (swelling) of the tissues of the small intestine and colon. Common IBDs include Crohn's disease and ulcerative colitis.

insulin: a hormone that regulates the body's ability to metabolize sugar. People with type 1 diabetes (which usually develops in childhood) lack insulin, so sugar builds up in their blood. In people with type 2 diabetes (which usually develops in adults), the body produces insulin but doesn't process it properly. Symptoms of diabetes include urinating a lot, being very hungry and thirsty, vision problems, weight loss, and fatigue.

Lactobacillus: a genus of bacteria that lives in the vagina and gut and that produces lactic acid, which helps babies digest breast milk

meningitis: an inflammation of the meninges (the protective membranes covering the brain and spinal cord) that can be caused by bacteria and viruses

metabolize: to process food and other substances to produce the materials and energy necessary for life

metagenomics: the study of genetic material of every microbe present in a laboratory sample. Metagenomics allows researchers to study a whole community of microbes, such as the microbes in a person's mouth.

methicillin-resistant *Staphylococcus aureus* (MRSA): a strain of *S. aureus* that over time has developed resistance to treatment by methicillin and by many other antibiotics

microorganism: an organism, such as a bacterium, that is too small to be seen without a microscope. Microorganisms are also called microbes.

mutation: a change in the DNA of an organism. Mutations can be beneficial to a microbe living in a human host, helping it better reproduce or survive. However, a mutation might be harmful to the organism's host. For instance, bacterial DNA might mutate to become antibiotic-resistant, preventing people from killing the bacteria with antibiotics.

mutualists: Microbes that benefit their human hosts and receive some benefit in return. Many microbes found in the human gut are mutualists. We give them food and a place to live, and in return, they help digest our food and fight harmful bacteria in the gut.

natural selection: the process, first proposed by naturalist Charles Darwin in 1859, by which organisms that are best adapted to their environment are more likely to survive and produce offspring

nucleus: a structure inside certain cells containing genetic material. Animal and plant cells have nuclei. Bacteria and archaea do not.

nutrient broth: a liquid in which researchers grow microorganisms

pathogen: a microbe such as a bacterium, fungus, or virus that can produce disease

penicillin: an antibiotic created from *Penicillium*, a genus of fungi. Developed in the 1940s, penicillin was the first antibiotic used successfully to treat diseases in human beings.

Penicillium: a genus of fungi. Some members of the genus produce penicillin, an antibiotic developed in the 1940s.

petri plate: a small, shallow plastic or glass dish, filled with a jellylike substance called agar. Scientists can culture (grow) bacteria and other substances inside petri plates.

plasmid: a small loop of genetic material inside a bacterial cell. Plasmids carry extra DNA that can be passed from bacterium to bacterium as part of horizontal gene transfer.

prebiotics: nutrients that promote the growth of beneficial microbes. Prebiotics occur naturally in foods such as asparagus, garlic, and onions.

probiotics: live microbes that are believed to provide health benefits, particularly to the digestive tract and the immune system. Probiotics are typically taken as a supplement in powder or pill form or are ingested through foods. Some foods, such as yogurt, naturally contain probiotics. Other foods contain probiotics added by manufacturers.

prokaryote: a living thing whose cells do not contain a nucleus. Bacteria and archaea are prokaryotes.

Propionibacterium acnes: bacteria that live on the skin and that are linked to acne in humans

protein: a large biological molecule that performs a vast array of functions within living organisms, such as bringing about chemical reactions and forming the structural material of hair and fingernails

resistance: the ability of a microorganism to survive exposure to a toxic agent (such as an antibiotic) formerly used to kill it

ribonucleic acid (RNA): a large molecule found inside cells that is essential for life. Each RNA molecule is a single strand of chemical units called nucleotides. RNA plays a central role in the protein-making process carried out in the cell by ribosomes.

ribosomes: large particles that are found inside cells and are the main protein-making apparatus of the cell. Each ribosome is spherical in shape and is made of RNA and proteins in roughly equal amounts.

16S ribosomal RNA gene: a gene that forms part of a ribosome in prokaryotes. The gene is slightly different in each prokaryote, so researchers use it as a genetic fingerprint to identify individual prokaryote species.

Staphylococcus aureus: bacteria that live on the skin and that can cause infection inside the body. Boils, abscesses, and food poisoning are some of the health problems caused by this bacterium.

Streptococcus haemolyticus: bacteria that live on the skin and that can cause infections of the heart, blood, and urinary tract

syphilis: a sexually transmitted disease caused by the bacterium *Treponema pallidum*

tuberculosis: an infection of the lungs caused by *Mycobacterium tuberculosis*

type 1 diabetes: an autoimmune disease that results from the destruction of insulin-producing cells in the pancreas. The lack of insulin leads to increased sugar in the blood and urine and can be life threatening. Type 1 diabetes typically surfaces when people are still young. Type 2 diabetes, which involves the insufficient production and processing of insulin, usually emerges in adulthood.

virus: infectious particles that are smaller than bacteria and can reproduce only inside a host cell. Viruses cause a range of diseases, including influenza, measles, and smallpox.

Western world: the industrialized cultures of North America and western Europe

SOURCE NOTES

14 Sandra Blakeslee, "Microbial Life's Steadfast Champion," *New York Times*, October 15, 1996, http://www.nytimes.com/1996/10/15/science/microbial-life-s-steadfast-champion.html?pagewanted=all&src=pm.

21 Clifford Dobell, *Antony Van Leeuwenhoek and His "Little Animals"* (New York: Dover Publications, 1960), 60.

22 Ibid.

23 Ibid.

35 Alexander Fleming, "Penicillin," Nobelprize.org, accessed February 2, 2015, http://www.nobelprize.org/nobel_prizes/medicine/laureates/1945/fleming-lecture.pdf.

37–38 Tara Parker-Pope, "Drug Resistance, Explained," *New York Times*, March 27, 2008, http://well.blogs.nytimes.com/2008/03/27/drug-resistance-explained/?_r=0, 71.

44 Carl Zimmer, "When You Swallow a Grenade," *National Geographic*, December 18, 2012, http://phenomena.nationalgeographic.com/2012/12/18/when-you-swallow-a-grenade.

47 "Antibiotic Resistance Threats in the United States, 2013," Centers for Disease Control and Prevention, accessed February 10, 2015, http://www.cdc.gov/drugresistance/pdf/ar-threats-2013-508.pd.

50 Susan Brink, "Why India Is a Hotbed of Antibiotic Resistance and Sweden Is Not," *National Public Radio*, September 17, 2015, http://www.npr.org/sections/goatsandsoda/2015/09/17/441146398/why-india-is-a-hotbed-of-antibiotic-resistance-and-sweden-is-not.

56 Gary Taubes, "David Relman," interview, Sciencewatch.com, September 9, 2009, http://archive.sciencewatch.com/inter/aut/2009/09-sep/09sepRelm.

58–59 Ibid.

62 "NIH Human Microbiome Project Defines Normal Bacterial Makeup of the Body," National Institutes of Health, June 13, 2012, http://www.nih.gov/news/health/jun2012/nhgri-13.htm.

67 Ed Yong, "Baby's First Bacteria Depend on Route of Delivery," *National Geographic*, June 23, 2010, http://phenomena.nationalgeographic.com/2010/06/23/babys-first-bacteria-depend-on-route-of-delivery.

76 Martin J. Blaser, *Missing Microbes: How the Overuse of Antibiotics Is Fueling Our Modern Plagues* (New York: Henry Holt, 2014), 116.

82 "Changes in the Gut Bacteria Protect against Stroke, Research Finds," *Science Daily*, December 14, 2012, http://www.sciencedaily.com/releases/2012/12/121214091024.htm.

82 Raphael Kellman, "Why the Microbiome Is Your Key to Glowing Skin & Healthy Weight," *Mindbodygreen*, March 14, 2015, http://www.mindbodygreen.com/0-17842/why-the-microbiome-is-your-key-to-glowing-skin-healthy-weight.html.

82 Richard Sprague, "Overselling the Microbiome," *Richard Sprague* (blog), June 26, 2015, http://blog.richardsprague.com/2015/06/overselling-microbiome.html.

82 Jonathan Eisen, "11+ Things Everyone Needs to Know about Microbes," MicroBEnet, August 2012, http://phylogenomics.blogspot.com/2012/08/the-microbiome-in-news-risk-of.htm.

85 Ed Yong, "Searching for a 'Healthy' Microbiome," *NOVA Next*, January 29, 2014, http://www.pbs.org/wgbh/nova/next/body/microbiome-diversity.

85 Ibid.

89 Carl Zimmer, "Antibiotics Have Turned Our Bodies from Gardens into Battlefields," *Wired*, April 3, 2014, http://www.wired.com/2014/04/martin-blaser-antibiotics.

89–90 "Antibiotic Resistance Threats," Centers for Disease Control and Prevention.

92 Blaser, *Missing Microbes*, 20.

SELECTED BIBLIOGRAPHY

"Antibiotic Resistance Threats in the United States, 2013." Centers for Disease Control and Prevention. Accessed February 10, 2015. http://www.cdc.gov/drugresistance/pdf/ar-threats-2013-508.pdf.

Conniff, Richard. "Microbes: The Trillions of Creatures Governing Your Health." *Smithsonian Magazine*, May 2013. http://www.smithsonianmag.com/science-nature/microbes-the-trillions-of-creatures-governing-your-health-37413457/?all&no-ist.

De Kruif, Paul. *Microbe Hunters*. San Diego: Harcourt, 1926.

Groopman, Jerome. "Superbugs." *New Yorker*, August 11, 2008. http://www.newyorker.com/magazine/2008/08/11/superbugs.

Harmon, Katherine. "Bugs Inside: What Happens When the Microbes That Keep Us Healthy Disappear?" *Scientific American*, December 16, 2009. http://www.scientificamerican.com/article/human-microbiome-change.

Koenig, J. E., A. Spor, N. Scalfone, A.D. Fricker, J. Stombaugh, R. Knight, L. T. Angenent, and R. E. Rey. "Succession of Microbial Consortia in the Developing Infant Gut Microbiome." *Proceedings of the National Academy of Sciences* 108 (2011): 4578–4585.

Lax, Eric. *The Mold in Dr. Florey's Coat: The Story of the Penicillin Miracle*. New York: Henry Holt, 2004.

McKenna, Maryn. "Imagining the Post-Antibiotic Future." FERNnews, November 20, 2013. https://medium.com/@fernnews/imagining-the-post-antibiotics-future-892b57499e77.

"NIH Human Microbiome Project Defines Normal Bacterial Makeup of the Body." National Institutes of Health, June 13, 2012. http://www.nih.gov/news/health/jun2012/nhgri-13.htm.

Pollan, Michael. "Some of My Best Friends Are Germs." *New York Times Magazine*, May 15, 2013. http://www.nytimes.com/2013/05/19/magazine/say-hello-to-the-100-trillion-bacteria-that-make-up-your-microbiome.html.

Reid, Ann, and Shannon Greene. "FAQ: Human Microbiome." American Academy of Microbiology. Accessed January 19, 2015. http://academy.asm.org/index.php/faq-series/5122-humanmicrobiome.

Yong, Ed. "An Introduction to the Microbiome." *National Geographic*, August 8, 2010. http://academy.asm.org/images/stories/documents/FAQ_Human_Microbiome.pdf.

Zimmer, Carl. "When You Swallow a Grenade." *National Geographic*, December 18, 2012. http://phenomena.nationalgeographic.com/2012/12/18/when-you-swallow-a-grenade.

FURTHER INFORMATION

Books

Abramovitz, Melissa. *Autoimmune Disorders*. Farmington Hills, MI: Lucent Books, 2011.

Blaser, Martin J. *Missing Microbes: How the Overuse of Antibiotics Is Fueling Our Modern Plagues*. New York: Henry Holt, 2014.

Dougherty, Terri. *Sexually Transmitted Diseases*. Farmington Hills, MI: Lucent Books, 2010.

Dunn, Rob. *The Wild Life of Our Bodies*. New York: HarperCollins, 2011.

Enders, Giulia. *Gut: The Inside Story of Our Most Underrated Organ*. Vancouver, BC: Greystone Books, 2015.

Farrell, Jeanette. *Invisible Allies: Microbes That Shape Our Lives*. New York: Square Fish Books, 2016.

Goldsmith, Connie. *Superbugs Strike Back: When Antibiotics Fail*. Minneapolis: Twenty-First Century Books, 2007.

Knight, Rob. *Follow Your Gut: The Enormous Impact of Tiny Microbes*. New York: Simon & Schuster, 2015.

McKenna, Maryn. *Superbug: The Fatal Menace of MRSA*. New York: Free Press, 2011.

Sachs, Jessica Snyder. *Good Germs, Bad Germs*. New York: Farrar, Straus and Giroux, 2007.

Sheen, Barbara. *Asthma*. Farmington Hills, MI: Lucent Books, 2011.

———. *MRSA*. Farmington Hills, MI: Lucent Books, 2011.

Watson, James. *The Double Helix: A Personal Account of the Discovery of the Structure of DNA*. New York: Touchstone, 2001.

Yount, Lisa. *Rosalind Franklin: Photographing Biomolecules*. New York: Chelsea House, 2011.

Websites

Alliance for the Prudent Use of Antibiotics (APUA)
http://www.tufts.edu/med/apua
The APUA promotes responsible use of antibiotics to contain drug resistance. Its website contains information for doctors, nurses, officials, and consumers about the proper use of antibiotics and the problem of resistance.

Human Microbiome

http://learn.genetics.utah.edu/content/microbiome/

This website, run by the Genetics Science Learning Center at the University of Utah, includes articles and videos about the role of microbes in health and disease, the problem of antibiotic resistance, and how scientists study the microbiome.

New Tree of Life

http://treeoflife.nmnaturalhistory.org/index.html

This interactive website from the New Mexico Museum of Natural History and Science explores the history of life and explains the relationships between bacteria, archaea, and eukaryotes.

Open Biome

http://www.openbiome.org

Visit this website to learn more about fecal microbiota transplants (FMT) and the process of stool donations.

The Power of Poop

http://thepowerofpoop.com

The Power of Poop is a patient resource center dedicated to promoting fecal microbiota transplant (FMT) and to raising awareness of the role of the human microbiome in digestive illness. The website provides information for both fecal donors and recipients.

Scientific American: The Crisis of Antibiotic Resistance

http://www.scientificamerican.com/report/antibiotic-resistance-bacteria-in-depth/

This website from *Scientific American* magazine features a range of in-depth articles on the problem of antibiotic resistance and the race for new antibiotics.

The Secret World Inside You

http://www.amnh.org/exhibitions/the-secret-world-inside-you

This website, a companion to an exhibit at the American Museum of Natural History, offers articles on our skin and gut microbiomes, as well as the microbes we acquire from our mothers at birth.

TED: Meet Your Microbes

https://www.ted.com/talks/jonathan_eisen_meet_your_microbes

This talk by microbiome researcher Jonathan Eisen shares what we know about the sea of microbes in and on our bodies and the surprising ways these microbes work.

INDEX

PHOTO ACKNOWLEDGMENTS

The images in this book are used with the permission of: © Photo Researchers RM/Getty Images, p. 7; © STEVE GSCHMEISSNER/Science Photo Library RM/Getty Images, p. 11; © iStockphoto.com/audaxl, p. 15; © Laura Westlund/ Independent Picture Service, pp. 16, 38, 40, 57, 63; © The Print Collector/ Alamy, pp. 21, 22; © Fotosearch/Stringer/Getty Images, p. 27; © Popperfoto/ Getty Images, p. 28; © SSPL/NMeM/Daily Herald Archive/Getty Images, p. 31; Image courtesy of The Advertising Archives, pp. 32, 35; © David M Phillips/Photo Researchers/Getty Images, p. 37; © R Parulan Jr./Flickr RF/Getty Images, p. 43; © Steve Woit/Design Pics/agency/Getty Images, p. 46; © Central Press/Hulton Archive/Getty Images, p. 53; © Dr. Kari Lounatmaa/Science Source, p. 55; © foto by Chandler Chou/Getty Images, p. 69; © UIG via Getty Images, p. 71; © Dennis Welsh/The Image Bank/Getty Images, p. 74; © George Steinmetz/Corbis, p. 79; © Nigel Dickinson/Alamy, p. 88.

Front cover: © S. Lowry/Univ Ulster/The Image Bank/Getty Images.

ABOUT THE AUTHOR

Rebecca E. Hirsch has written about science and discovery in dozens of books for children and young adults. A former scientist, she holds a PhD in cellular and molecular biology from the University of Wisconsin. Rebecca lives in State College, Pennsylvania, with her husband, Rick; their three daughters; various pets; and many thousands of species of microbes. You can learn more at her website: www.rebeccahirsch.com.